Capitalization & Punctuation

Spelling & Vocabulary

How to Use This Book

What makes *Games Galore—Language Arts* as exciting for you as it is for your students? The easy-to-use organization, of course! Each game is designed with the following features:

- **Skill:** Identify the skill in a snap.
- **Number of players:** Quickly note partner, small-group, and whole-class games.
- **Materials:** Round up needed supplies based on this handy reference.
- **Object of the game:** Decide if a game provides the skill practice your students need.
- **Playing the game:** Cleverly written to the student, these directions are printed on a white background so you can easily copy them and place them with the game for student reference.

Some of the games will contain the following to make preparation or play even easier!

- **Reproducible page(s):** With many games, you'll find a timesaving reproducible—such as a student record sheet, gameboard, or pattern—located on the page following the game description.
- **Teacher preparation:** If there is advanced preparation needed to set up the game, refer to these step-by-step instructions.
- **Variation:** Extend the life of a game by adjusting the rules, setup, skill, or difficulty.
- **Answer keys:** While many games rely on student knowledge and teacher monitoring, you will find necessary answer keys at the back of the book for handy reference.

Grades
1-3

LANGUAGE ARTS

Why practice key curriculum skills using games? Games provide the perfect opportunity for students to engage in active learning, take part in social interactions, and—let's not forget—have fun!

With literacy standards in mind, we designed each game in *Games Galore—Language Arts* to add purpose to students' play. Through hands-on, partner, small-group, and whole-class games, your students will review key literacy concepts as well as foster communication, cooperation, problem-solving, and critical-thinking skills.

Games Galore—Language Arts is also designed to save you time. The comprehensive table of contents conveniently lists each game by skill, so you can quickly find a perfect fit for your curriculum needs. Plus "How to Use This Book" (page 4) will familiarize you with the book's helpful design and easy-to-use contents. Enjoy, and let the games begin!

©2002 by THE EDUCATION CENTER, INC.
All rights reserved.
ISBN #1-56234-494-3

Manufactured in the United States

10 9 8 7 6 5 4 3 2 1

Table of Contents

Tic-Tac-Toe, Three Sounds in a Row

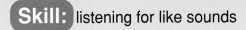

Skill: listening for like sounds

Number of players: 2

Materials:
- copy of one tic-tac-toe gameboard (page 6) for each pair
- 5 matching game markers for each player (different color or style per child)
- small paper bag filled with a set of picture cards for each player (page 7)

Teacher preparation:
Cut apart a set of picture cards for each player. Place each set in a separate bag.

Object of the game:
to be the first to get three markers in a row vertically, horizontally, or diagonally and then call out "Tic-tac-toe, three sounds in a row" to win the game

Playing the game:
1. Player 1 randomly draws two cards from his bag and says each picture's name. If the beginning sounds match, the player puts a game marker on the first gameboard. If they do not match, his turn ends.
2. He lays his used cards facedown in a stack in front of him. If the discarded cards are needed to continue play, have each player shuffle his cards and put them back in his bag.
3. Players take turns until one gets three game markers in a row up and down, across, or diagonally and is the first to call out "Tic-tac-toe, three sounds in a row."

Gameboards

Player X: _____

Player O: _____

Player X: _____

Player O: _____

Player X: _____

Player O: _____

Player X: _____

Player O: _____

Sounds Like P...P...Popcorn

Skill: listening for like sounds

Number of players: whole class (divided into two teams)

Materials for each group:

- 2 prepared sets of colored index cards (1 color for each team, 1 card for each player)
- word list (on this page)
- resealable plastic bag
- bag of popped popcorn
- 20 popcorn kernels
- 3 small bowls

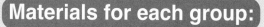

Teacher preparation:

1. For one set of index cards, use a marker to label each card with a different letter. (Choose as many beginning consonants as needed from the list at the right.) Label the second set of cards to match the first set.
2. Put ten popcorn kernels in a bowl for each team.
3. Put 20 pieces of popcorn in the third bowl. Display all three bowls at the front of the classroom.
4. Divide the class into two seated teams and then distribute the cards (one color for each team, one card for each player).

Object of the game:

to be the first team to "pop" its bowl of popcorn by correctly identifying ten like initial sounds

ball
dog
fork
gas
hot
little
mud
note
pail
race
sand
turtle
vest
water
yellow
zoo

Playing the game:

1. As the teacher reads a word from the list, both teams listen for the initial sound.
2. The first player from either team to say "Pop!" when he hears a word that starts with his letter replaces one popcorn kernel from his team's bowl with a popped piece. He puts the kernel in a resealable bag and leaves it near the bowls.
3. The first team to successfully replace all ten popcorn kernels with ten popped pieces wins the game. Both teams enjoy the remaining popcorn as a treat!

©The Education Center, Inc.

Variation:

Replace words in the list as needed; then play the game with final sounds.

All Aboard the Alphaboard!

Skill: matching beginning sounds with initial consonants

Number of players: 2–4

Materials:
- prepared alphaboard gameboard for each pair or small group
- game marker for each player
- die for each pair or small group

Teacher preparation:
Assemble the gameboard before distributing.

Object of the game:
to be the first to reach the finish line by matching letters and beginning sounds

Playing the game:
1. Player 1 rolls the die and moves her game marker that number of spaces along the railroad track.
2. The player reads aloud the letter name on which her game marker lands.
3. She selects a picture on the gameboard that has the same initial letter sound and then says its name. The other players indicate whether she is correct. If she is correct, she keeps her place on the gameboard. If she is incorrect, she moves her game marker back two spaces.
4. The first player to reach the finish line wins the game.

Variation:

When a student selects a picture and says its name, have her name a second word that begins with the same sound.

ALPHA

START
b
d
f
h
j
k
l
m
n
p
r
s
t
v
w
x
y
z
b
d
f
h
j
k
l
m
n
p
q
r
s
t
Be Mine
LIBERTY
IN GOD WE TRUST
1990

Cut here.

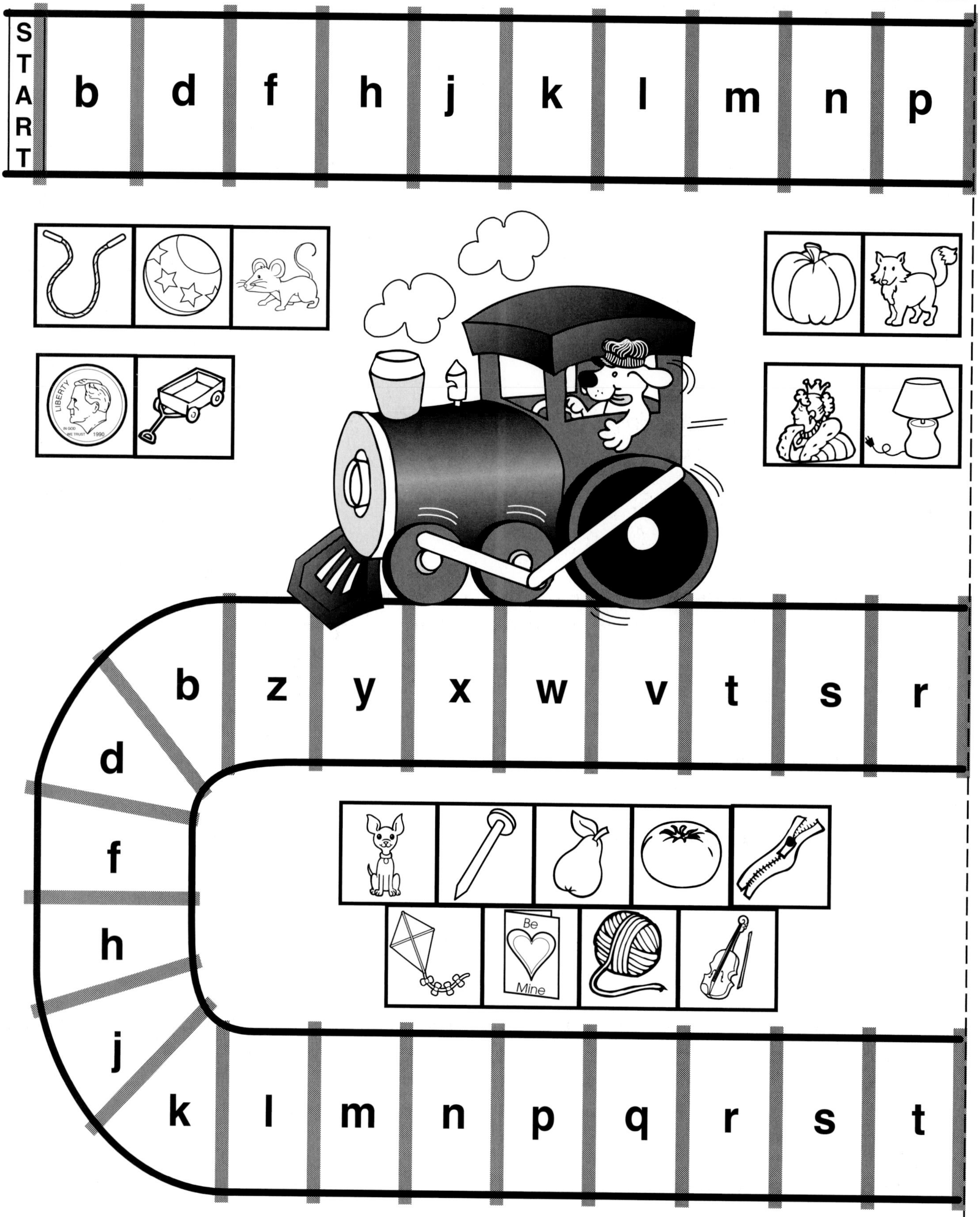

BOARD

Cut on the dotted line on page 10. Squeeze a thin line of glue in the gray area of section B on this page. Glue the cut edge of section A on top of the gray area.

q r s t v w x y z b c d f g

h j k l m n p q

v w x y z b d f g

FINISH

B

Chips

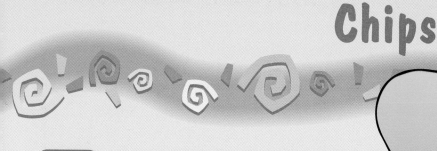

Skill: identifying letter-sound relationships

Number of players: 4

Materials:
- copy of page 13 for each group
- copy of page 14 for each player
- jumbo paper clip for each group
- pencil for each group
- 48 plastic chips for each group

Teacher preparation:

Demonstrate how to spin the paper clip indicator by placing it around a pencil point positioned at the center of the spinner.

Object of the game:

to be the first person on each team to cover all the pictures on his gameboard by correctly identifying ending letter-sound relationships

Playing the game:
1. Each player counts 12 chips and puts them near his gameboard.
2. In turn, each player spins the spinner and then reads aloud the number and the letter on which the paper clip lands.
3. The player looks for that number of pictures on his gameboard with the matching final sound.
4. The player puts a chip on each matching picture. After he places the chip(s), or if he can't place any, play moves to the next player.
5. The first player to cover all of the pictures on his gameboard wins the game.

©The Education Center, Inc.

Variation:

Reprogram the spinner to play the game with initial sounds.
Write *h, d, f, w* on spaces with a "1" and *l, s, c, b* on spaces with a "2."

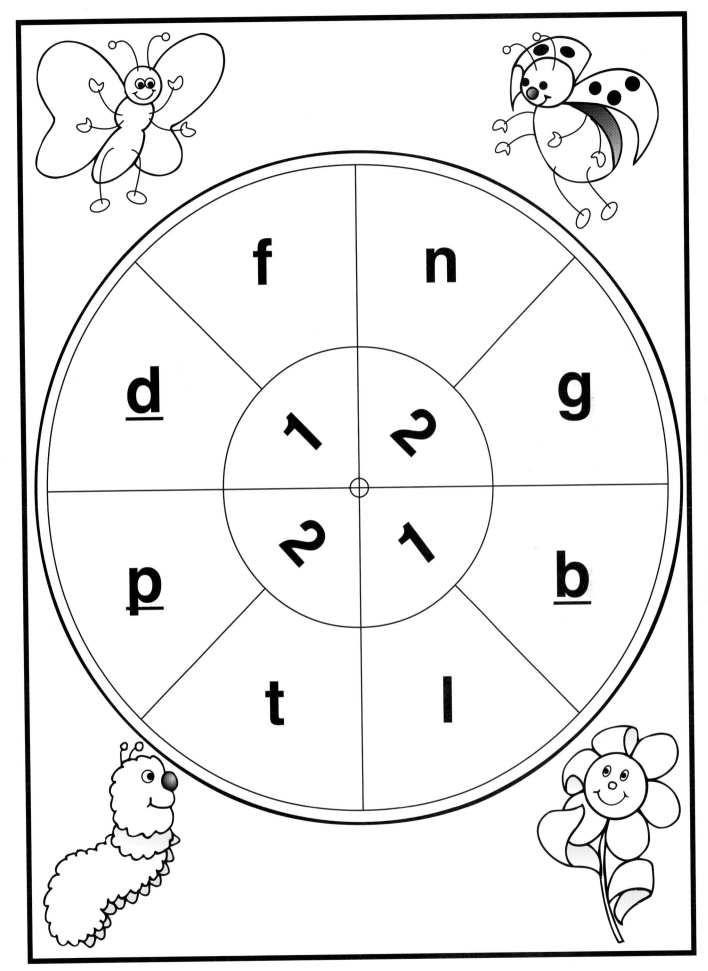

Rhyme Time

Skill: pairing rhyming words

Number of players: 4

Materials:
- 50 prepared index card halves

Teacher preparation:
1. Write a list of 25 pairs of rhyming words on a sheet of paper (for example, *cat, hat; fan, man*).
2. Cut 25 index cards in half. Write one word from the list on each card.

Object of the game:
to get the most cards by matching rhyming words.

Playing the game:
1. One player shuffles the cards and then lays five cards faceup on the playing surface. She places the rest of the cards facedown in a stack.
2. She reads the five cards. If she finds any two that rhyme, she moves them to her side of the playing area.
3. Then she continues her turn by drawing a card from the top of the stack, reading the word shown, and checking to see whether it rhymes with any of the remaining words displayed on the table.
4. If she finds a rhyming word, she moves the two cards off to the side and draws again. If not, she lays the card faceup on the table with the other cards.
5. The next player repeats Steps 3 and 4. Players continue taking turns until all of the cards in the stack have been used.
6. The player with the most cards wins.

Variation:
In order to count a rhyming word pair as a match, the player has to think of and then say a third rhyming word. If she cannot, the match remains on the table until either she or an opponent is able to do so.

Time Those Rhymes

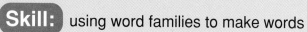

Skill: using word families to make words

Number of players: 2–4

Materials:
- die from page 17 for each group
- pencil for each player
- sheet of white paper for each player
- 1-minute timer for each group

Teacher preparation:

Cut out and assemble the die pattern.

Object of the game:

write the most words for each word family rolled

Playing the game:

1. To play a round, one player rolls the die, reads the word family aloud, and starts the timer.
2. Each player writes as many words using the rolled word family as he can in one minute.
3. The player who correctly writes the most rhyming words wins the round.
4. To play a new round, repeat Steps 1–3. If the die lands on a previously used word family, the player rolls again.
5. Play continues until each word family has been rolled.

©The Education Center, Inc.

Variation:

Play an elimination version! One player rolls the die. Each player, in turn, names a word using the corresponding word family. The first player who can't think of a new word is out. Play continues until only one player remains.

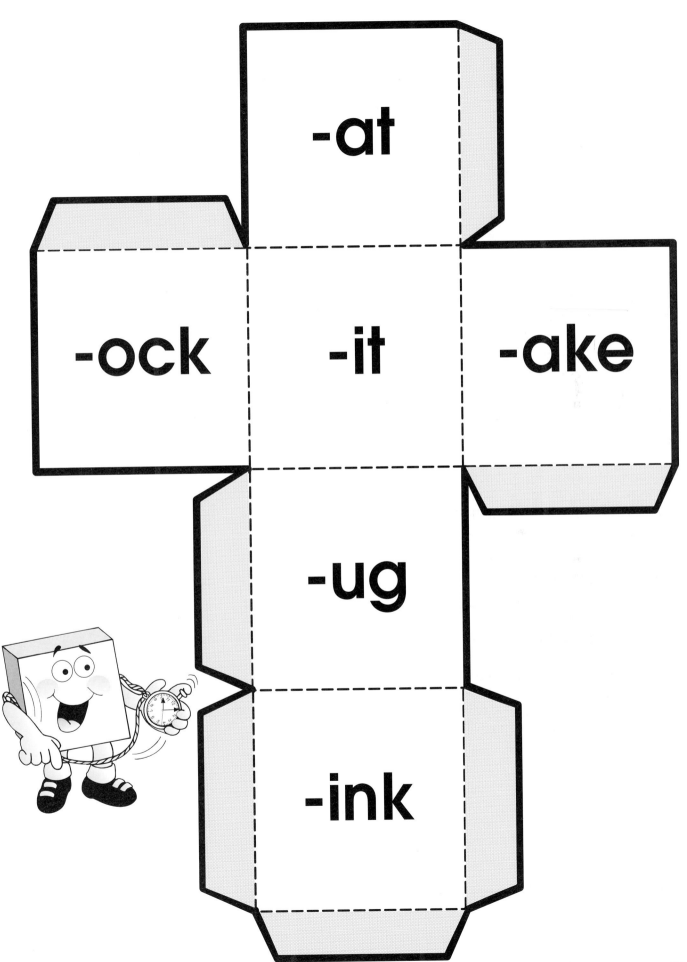

-at

-ock -it -ake

-ug

-ink

Word-Family Toss and Roll

Skill: using word families to make words

Number of players: 2

Materials:

- copy of pages 19 and 20 for each pair
- 2 game markers for each pair
- die for each pair
- sheet of paper for each player
- pencil for each player

Object of the game:

to be the player who creates more words using given onsets and rimes

Playing the game:

1. Each player puts his game marker on Start.
2. Player 1 rolls the die and then moves his marker along the gameboard according to the number rolled. He calls out the onset he lands on.
3. He looks at the word-family chart and chooses a rime that, when combined with his onset, will make a word. He writes the word on his paper. Player 2 confirms the word. If the word is correct, Player 2 takes a turn. If the word is incorrect, Player 1 must draw a line through it. Each player may write each word only once.
4. Play continues until one player crosses the finish line. Each player counts the words on his list, not including those that have a line drawn through them. The player with the highest total number of words wins.

Variation:

Draw a six-block word-family chart and program each block with one of the following rimes: *-ell, -op, -ore, -ice, -ash,* and *-ill.* Invite students to play the game using both charts.

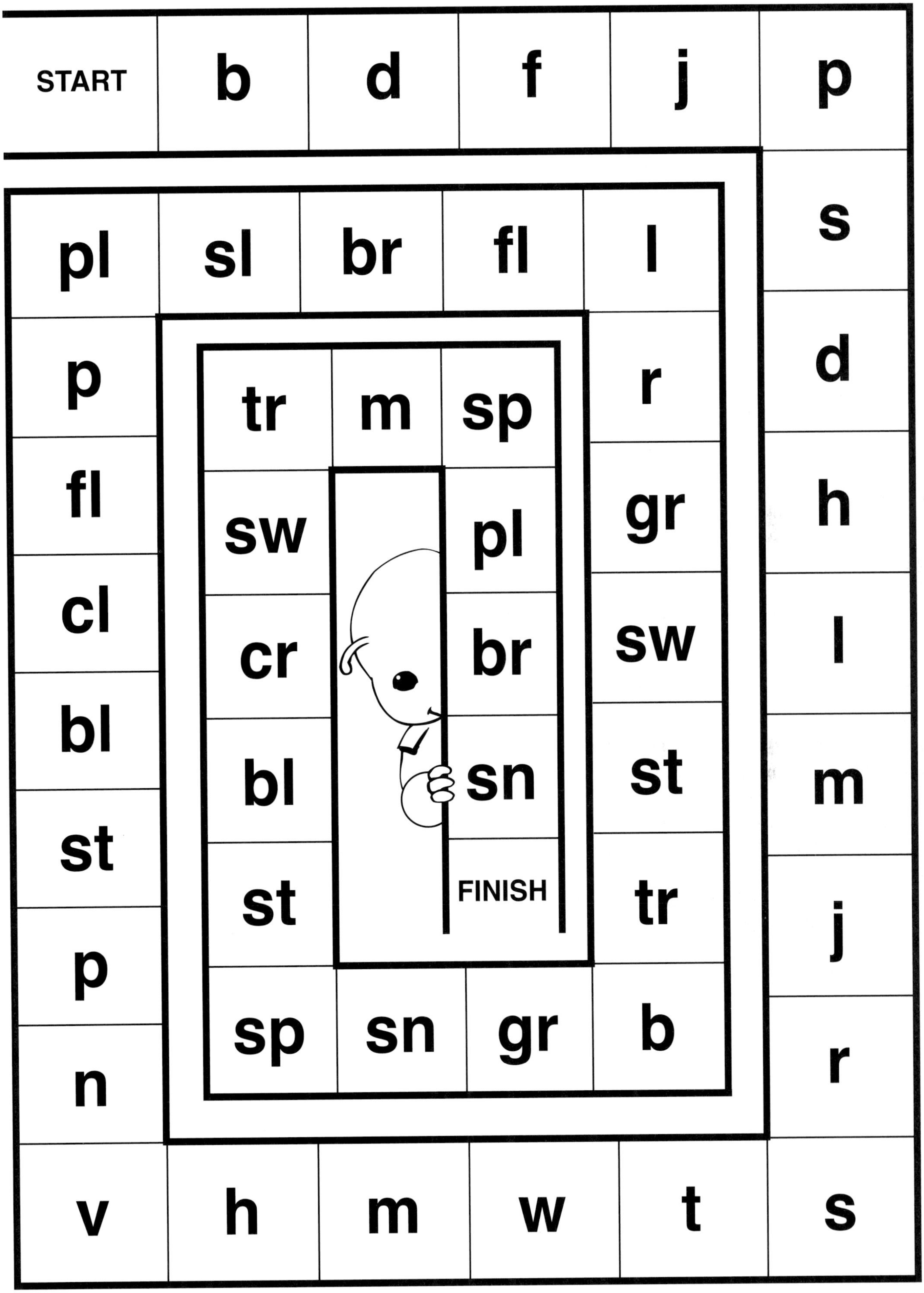
START
b
d
f
j
p
s
d
h
l
m
j
r
s
t
w
m
h
v
n
p
st
bl
cl
fl
p
pl
sl
br
fl
l
r
gr
sw
st
tr
b
gr
sn
sp
st
bl
cr
sw
tr
m
sp
pl
br
sn
FINISH

Word-Family Chart

-at	-eat	-ock
-ing	-ake	-ot
-est	-in	-ug

Give Me Five!

Skill: naming rhyming words

Number of players: 2

Materials for each pair:
- sheets of white paper
- 2 pencils
- 2 pairs of scissors
- 1 prepared word card
- pair of dice

Teacher preparation:

Program each of four index cards with a different vocabulary word, such as *hat, say, fill, let, got,* or *old.* Be sure each word has at least eight words that rhyme with it.

Object of the game:

to be the first to label all five fingers with rhyming words.

Playing the game:
1. Each player traces one of her hands onto the white paper, cuts out the tracing, and then writes her name on the palm of the cutout.
2. Each pair receives one word card.
3. She writes the word shown on the thumb of her cutout.
4. Each player rolls a die. The player with the higher number writes a word on one finger that rhymes with the word on the thumb.
5. Repeat Step 4 until one player has a rhyming word written on each of the five fingers. A word cannot be repeated during a round.
6. If time allows, play a second round. Each pair trades word cards with another pair that does not have the same word. Then each player flips her cutout over and writes on the back.

Variation:

Use picture cards rather than word cards.

Silly Syllable Game

Skill: identifying syllables

Number of players: 2

Materials for each player:
- container
- 10 assorted objects (prize box items or manipulatives)
- 5 index cards numbered 1–5

Teacher preparation:
1. For each player, put ten assorted objects in one container.
2. Number five index cards for each player.

Object of the game:
to be the first player to correctly identify the number of syllables in the names of ten objects

Playing the game:
1. Each player lays her number cards end to end.
2. At the same time, each player randomly takes an object from her container. She places it below the card showing the number of syllables in the object's name.
3. Repeat Step 2 until each player has placed all of her objects below the cards.
4. With the help of the teacher, each child checks her answers. Correctly placed objects remain in place, while incorrectly placed objects are returned to their container. The player with more correct answers wins.

Variation:

In turn, have each player select two objects and lay them below the corresponding cards. Then have him write and solve a math problem using the number of syllables as the numbers in the equation. For example, if the items selected are a car (one syllable) and an eraser (three syllables), a possible equation would be $1 + 3 = 4$.

Ski Mt. Syllable

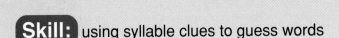

Skill: using syllable clues to guess words

Number of players: 2–4

Materials:
- copy of page 24 for each small group (cut apart)
- copy of page 25 for each pair or small group
- copy of the answer key (page 95) for each pair or small group.
- die for each pair or small group
- marker for each player

Object of the game:

to be the first player to "ski" to the bottom of Mt. Syllable by correctly solving the most syllable clues

Playing the game:

1. One player shuffles the cards and stacks them facedown on the playing surface.
2. Each player sets his game marker on Start.
3. Player 1 rolls the die and moves that number of spaces. Then he draws the top card and reads aloud the syllable number and clue. He thinks of an answer with the number of syllables listed.
4. If Player 1's answer is incorrect, he moves back one space and his turn ends. If his answer is correct, he stays where he is.
5. If a player draws a card that reads "Move back…" or "Move ahead…" he must do as the card reads and his turn ends.
6. The first player to get to the bottom of Mt. Syllable wins.

Variation:

For an added challenge, each time a student gives an answer, have him also name a word that has one more syllable than his answer. If his answer is correct, have him move ahead one more space.

First on the ski lift! Move ahead 1 space.	**1** opposite of cold 1.	**3** game with a hoop and net 2.	**3** trip a family takes 3.
Ski lift broken. Move back 3 spaces.	**2** large salty body of water 4.	**3** caterpillar turns into a… 5.	**2** help you see better 6.
Lost ski poles. Move back 2 spaces.	**2** opposite of noisy 7.	**3** last name of first president of the United States 8.	**1** shoe for skiing 9.
Wearing warm gloves! Move ahead 2 spaces.	**3** month to celebrate Christmas 10.	**2** game with black-and-white ball 11.	**2** not afternoon or night 12.
Skiing too fast! Move ahead 3 spaces.	**3** animal in Australia that hops 13.	**1** opposite of fast 14.	**3** weekend day 15.
2 tastes good on french fries 16.	**2** house made of ice 17.	**2** room at the top of a house 18.	**2** opposite of uphill 19.

Ski Mt. Syllable

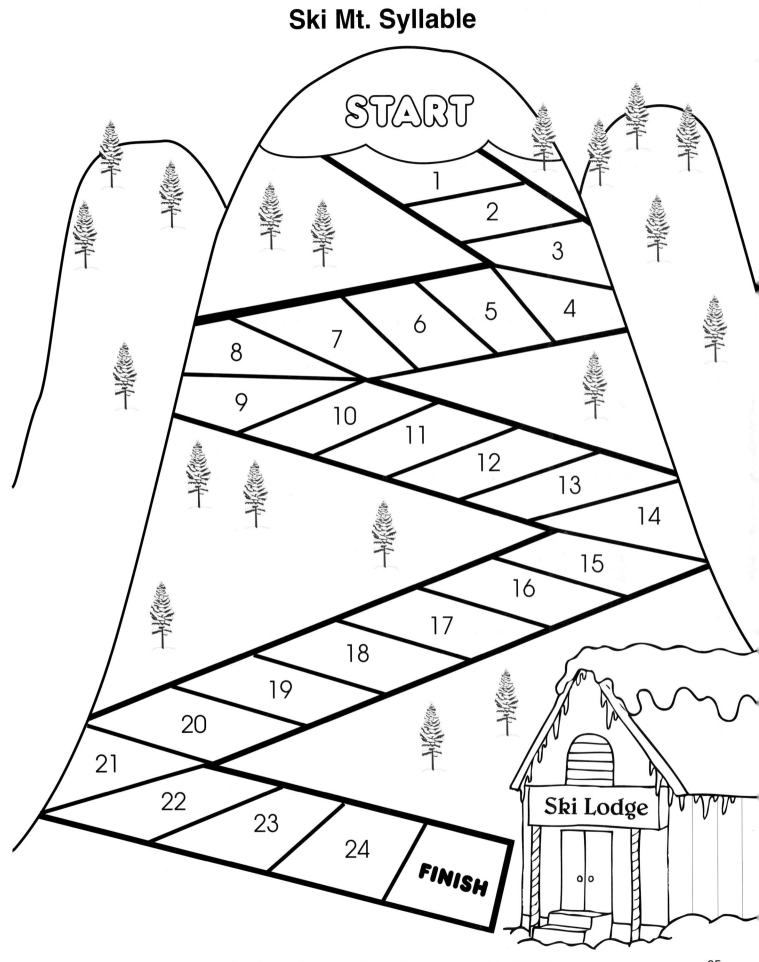

START

1
2
3
4
5
6
7
8
9
10
11
12
13
14
15
16
17
18
19
20
21
22
23
24

FINISH

Ski Lodge

Duck Detective

Skill: identifying syllabication rules

Number of players: 2

Materials for each pair:
- copy of game cards on page 27 (cut apart)
- copy of clue card on page 27
- copy of answer key on page 27

Object of the game:
to correctly identify more syllabication rules and collect more word cards

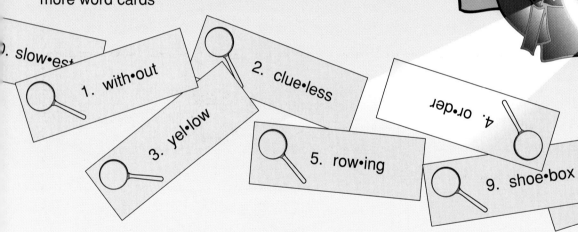

0. slow•est
1. with•out
2. clue•less
3. yel•low
4. or•der
5. row•ing
6. d___town
7. c
8. of•ten
9. shoe•box

Playing the game:
1. Detective 1 shuffles the cards and places the stack facedown on the playing surface.
2. Detective 1 draws the top card and reads aloud the word.
3. He studies the clue card and chooses the best rule for the word on his card.
4. Detective 2 refers to the key to check the answer. If the answer is correct, Detective 1 keeps the card. If the answer is incorrect, he places the card on the bottom of the deck.
5. Detective 2 takes a turn.
6. Play continues until there are no more cards in the deck. The detective with more cards is the winner.

©The Education Center, Inc.

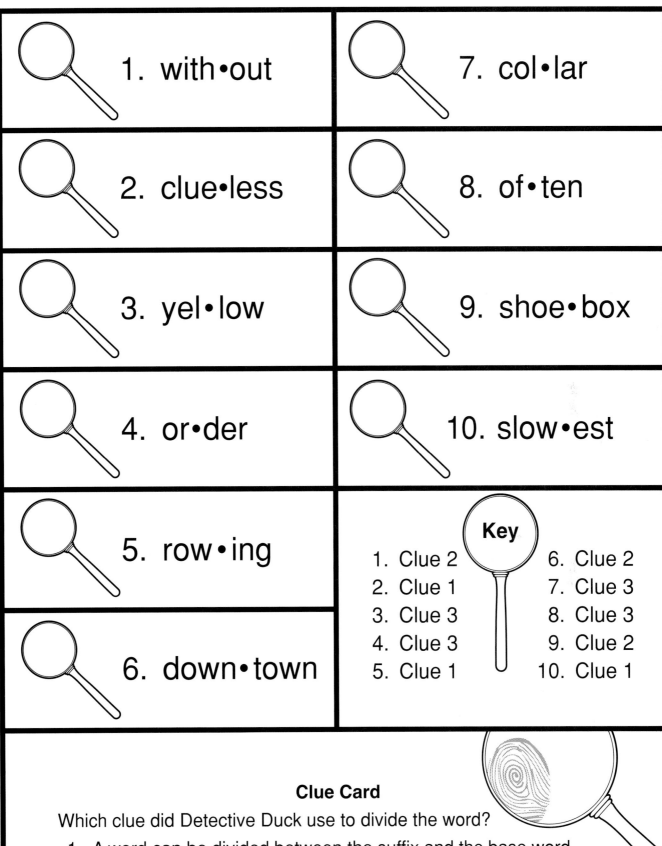

1. with•out

2. clue•less

3. yel•low

4. or•der

5. row•ing

6. down•town

7. col•lar

8. of•ten

9. shoe•box

10. slow•est

Key

1. Clue 2	6. Clue 2
2. Clue 1	7. Clue 3
3. Clue 3	8. Clue 3
4. Clue 3	9. Clue 2
5. Clue 1	10. Clue 1

Clue Card

Which clue did Detective Duck use to divide the word?

1. A word can be divided between the suffix and the base word.
2. A compound word can be divided between the two smaller words.
3. A word can be divided between two consonants in the middle.

Person, Place, or Thing-A-Ma-Jig

Skill: identifying and using nouns

Number of players: 2–4

Materials for each group:
- copy of pages 29 and 30
- resealable plastic bag

Teacher preparation:
1. Cut apart the word cards.
2. Cut out the gameboards.
3. Store the word cards and gameboards in the resealable bag.

Object of the game:
to be the first player to correctly label three nouns in a row.

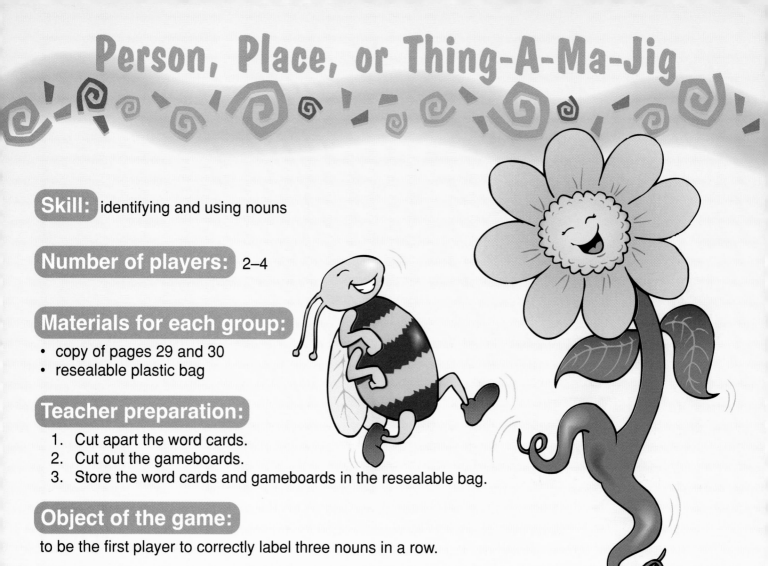

Playing the game:
1. A player distributes one gameboard to each player and then shuffles the word cards and lays them facedown on the playing surface.
2. Player 1 draws a card. She decides if the card names a person, place, or thing and then lays it on a matching space on her gameboard.
3. If she draws a word card that is not a person, place, or thing, she loses a turn.
4. Players take turns until one player covers three spaces in a row across, up and down, or diagonally.

©The Education Center, Inc.

Variation:

Once a student identifies the word shown on the word card as a person, place, or thing, have her correctly use the noun in a sentence before placing the card on her gameboard. If the sentence is incorrect, the student places the card at the bottom of the stack.

Word Cards

boy	school	bike	girl	garden	car
man	bakery	pencil	woman	house	cup
mother	store	heart	uncle	bedroom	clock
aunt	bathroom	tree	sister	bank	flower
brother	yard	bee	teacher	fair	star
skip	hop	crawl	do	cry	sing
run	eat	sit	write	fill	read

Gameboards

place	person	thing
person	thing	place
thing	place	person

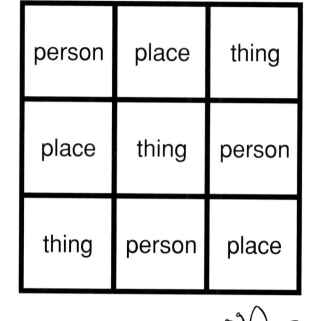

person	place	thing
place	thing	person
thing	person	place

person	thing	place
place	person	thing
thing	place	person

thing	person	place
person	place	thing
place	thing	person

Noun Town

Skill: naming nouns

Number of players: 2–4

Materials:
- copy of page 32 for each group (cut apart)
- copy of page 33 for each group
- copy of the answer key on page 95
- game marker for each player

Object of the game:

to be the first player to correctly name the most nouns and reach the finish line

Playing the game:

1. Each player puts his game marker on Start. One player shuffles and then lays the game cards facedown on the playing surface.
2. Player 1 draws a card. He reads aloud the words on the card and then tells which word is a noun.
3. Player 2 refers to the answer key to confirm the answer. If the answer is correct, Player 1 moves ahead the number of spaces shown on the card. If the answer is incorrect, Player 1 does not move.
4. Players take turns until one player crosses Finish and wins the game.

Variation:

Before he can move ahead, each player must use all three of the words on his card in a sentence.

1. hot spinning snowman — Ahead 1	6. woman red think — Ahead 3	11. little bird adds — Ahead 2	16. Dr. Kay salty — Ahead 1	21. dry forgets school — Ahead 3
2. cheered teacher squeaky — Ahead 2	7. acted dark fairgrounds — Ahead 1	12. wet must home — Ahead 3	17. would straight suitcase — Ahead 2	22. hospital born gray — Ahead 1
3. forest two blew — Ahead 3	8. tall desk were — Ahead 2	13. mother crawl sticky — Ahead 1	18. beach thick washed — Ahead 3	23. round hammer counted — Ahead 2
4. explored thread loud — Ahead 1	9. Mr. Lee walked dirty — Ahead 3	14. hungry crayon draw — Ahead 2	19. eats boy six — Ahead 1	24. finally been classroom — Ahead 3
5. pink bought fireman — Ahead 2	10. could sweet mountains — Ahead 1	15. making tiny jungle — Ahead 3	20. bottle shall shiny — Ahead 2	25. called good child — Ahead 1

32

Noun Town

START

FINISH

Professor Pronoun

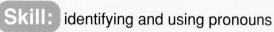

Skill: identifying and using pronouns

Number of players: 2–4

Materials:
- copy of page 35 for each group
- die for each group
- game marker for each player

Object of the game:

to be the first to reach Professor Pronoun's desk by correctly stating sentences containing pronouns

Playing the game:
1. Each player places her game marker on Start.
2. Player 1 rolls the die and moves her game marker that number of spaces.
3. She reads aloud the word written on the space. If the word on the space is a noun, the player loses her turn and moves back to her previous position.
4. If the word is a pronoun, she uses it in a sentence. If her sentence is correct, she stays where she is. If it is incorrect, she moves back to her previous position.
5. The first player to reach or pass Professor Pronoun's desk wins.

©The Education Center, Inc.

Variation:

For each turn, have the player select a second pronoun from the gameboard to include in her sentence. Both pronouns must be used correctly for the sentence to count.

START

| he | she | tree | her | dog | we |

us

I

you

| me | him | star | they | it | me | truck |

them

boy

we

| bee | her | us | he | she |

Professor
Pronoun

Professor
Pronoun

Treasure Chest of Pronouns

Skill: correctly naming pronouns

Number of players: 2

Materials for each pair:
- copy of page 37
- copy of the answer key on page 95
- number die
- 2 game markers

Object of the game:

to be the first player to correctly name pronouns and reach the treasure chest

Playing the game:

1. Each player lays her game marker on the parrot.
2. Player 1 rolls the die and moves her game marker that number of spaces.
3. She reads aloud the noun(s) written on the coin. (In some cases there will be a noun and a pronoun.)
4. She names a pronoun to replace the noun(s) on the coin. Player 2 refers to the key to confirm the answer. If her answer is incorrect, Player 1 moves back one space.
5. The first player to reach the treasure chest wins the game.

©The Education Center, Inc.

Variation:

Give each player a sheet of paper and a pencil. Each time she names a pronoun, have her write a sentence that includes it.

Treasure Chest of Pronouns

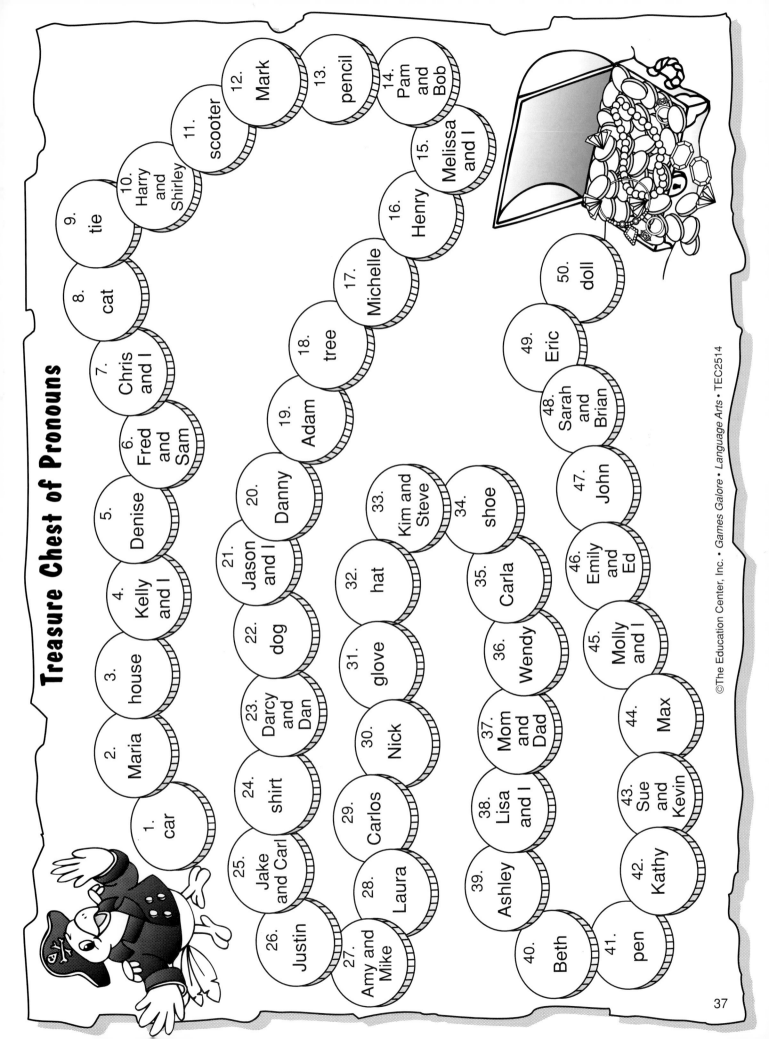

1. car
2. Maria
3. house
4. Kelly and I
5. Denise
6. Fred and Sam
7. Chris and I
8. cat
9. tie
10. Harry and Shirley
11. scooter
12. Mark
13. pencil
14. Pam and Bob
15. Melissa and I
16. Henry
17. Michelle
18. tree
19. Adam
20. Danny
21. Jason and I
22. dog
23. Darcy and Dan
24. shirt
25. Jake and Carl
26. Justin
27. Amy and Mike
28. Laura
29. Carlos
30. Nick
31. glove
32. hat
33. Kim and Steve
34. shoe
35. Carla
36. Wendy
37. Mom and Dad
38. Lisa and I
39. Ashley
40. Beth
41. pen
42. Kathy
43. Sue and Kevin
44. Max
45. Molly and I
46. Emily and Ed
47. John
48. Sarah and Brian
49. Eric
50. doll

Act-It-Out Verbs

Skill: acting out and guessing action verbs

Number of players: 3 or 4

Materials:

- three 3" x 5" index cards for each player
- 1-minute timer for each group
- paper and pencil for each group

Teacher preparation:

Write an action verb on each index card. Program enough cards for each player to get three cards.

Object of the game:

to earn the most points by successfully acting out and guessing action verbs

Playing the game:

1. Place the deck of verb cards facedown on the playing surface.
2. Player 1 draws a card from the top of the deck and sets the timer for one minute. Player 1 acts out the verb without speaking.
3. The other players try to guess the verb within the one-minute time limit. If a player guesses the verb correctly, he scores a point and so does Player 1. The verb card is set aside. If the verb is not guessed within the time limit, no points are awarded and the card is placed on the bottom of the deck.
4. The players continue taking turns until all cards are successfully guessed.
5. The player with the most points at the end of the game wins.

©The Education Center, Inc.

Variation:

Play the game as a whole class. Divide the class into groups and distribute a verb card to each group. Give groups three minutes to prepare. Then have one group at a time act out its verb in a pantomime skit. Award points to groups that successfully act out and guess the verbs.

Verb Safari

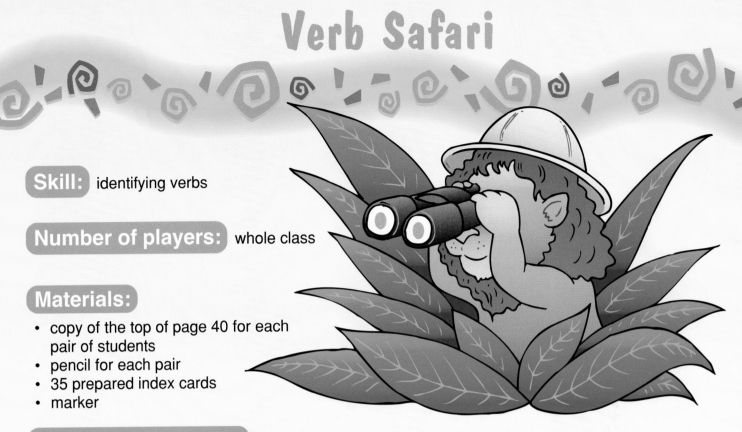

Skill: identifying verbs

Number of players: whole class

Materials:
- copy of the top of page 40 for each pair of students
- pencil for each pair
- 35 prepared index cards
- marker

Teacher preparation:
1. Using the list on page 40, write a different word on each of 35 index cards.
2. While students are out of the classroom, place the index cards around the classroom in locations where they are partially hidden.
3. Discuss these safari ground rules with your students:
    - Use quiet safari voices so you don't scare the verbs away!
    - Do not run. As true safari goers, walk slowly to take in all the sights!
    - Do not touch the verbs when you find them because they may bite!

Object of the game:

to find and list the most verbs in the allotted time

Playing the game:
1. The teacher announces the start of the verb safari. Student pairs search the room for verbs.
2. When a verb is found, the players record it on the word safari sheet.
3. If a word other than a verb is spotted, players simply continue searching for verbs.
4. The teacher announces the end of the safari.
5. The pair with the most correctly recorded verbs wins.

©The Education Center, Inc.

Variation:

Give each pair of verb hunters a sheet of writing paper along with the reproducible sheet. Have pairs write a complete sentence for each verb as it is found. The pair with the most sentences wins.

Names _____

Verb Safari

1. _____
2. _____
3. _____
4. _____
5. _____
6. _____
7. _____
8. _____

9. _____
10. _____
11. _____
12. _____
13. _____
14. _____
15. _____
16. _____

rake	wipe	think	pie
grab	poke	pack	student
pinch	eat	grin	planet
sit	teach	run	fresh
nod	float	walk	marker
sing	crawl	pay	barn
bump	clap	look	hamster
jump	scrub	grow	boy
skate	trade	skip	sheep

Hammer Grammar

Skill: recognizing subjects and verbs

Number of players: 2

Materials for each pair:

- the following prepared items from page 42:
  2 gameboards, 14 wood block cards
- 16 game markers (8 of a matching color for each player)
- prepared spinner
- pencil
- paper clip

The subject is Kevin!

Hammer Gramm...

Kevin saw a big dog.

Teacher preparation:

1. Cut out the gameboards and wood block cards.
2. In the attic space, label one gameboard "subject" and the other "verb."
3. Visually divide a six-inch paper plate in half with a marker, labeling one half "subject" and the other half "verb."
4. Show students how to complete the spinner using the pencil and paper clip.

Object of the game:

to identify subjects and verbs to complete three in a row

Playing the game:

1. Put the gameboards, wood block cards, and spinner in the playing area.
2. Player 1 spins the spinner.
3. Player 1 draws a wood block card, reads it aloud, and finds the subject or verb as indicated by the spin.
4. If Player 1 is correct, she places a game marker in any empty block on the matching house. If there are no open spaces, or if her answer is incorrect, she loses her turn. The card is returned to the bottom of the deck.
5. Player 2 takes a turn. When any player forms a row of three, she receives a point. Play continues until both gameboards are filled.
6. The player with more points wins the game. If tied, clear the gameboards and play until a player forms a row of three and wins the game.

©The Education Center, Inc.

Raul swam in a pool.

Oscar rode on a yellow bus.

My brother plays baseball.

Sam kicked the football.

My dad built this house.

Paul makes great cookies.

Baxter slept in his doghouse.

The sun set behind the hill.

My uncle works at the bank.

Students write in notebooks.

The nurse helps the doctor.

Mia learned Spanish.

Kevin saw a big dog.

The apple fell off the tree.

Hammer Grammar

©The Education Center, Inc. • Games Galore • Language Arts • TEC2514

Password

Skill: identifying nouns and verbs

Number of players: whole class

Materials for the whole class:

- 4 labeled containers (baskets or boxes)
- class supply of prepared 3" x 5" index cards
- chalkboard
- chalk

Teacher preparation:

1. Write a noun or verb on each card (see lists).
2. Label two containers "VERBS" and the other two "NOUNS."
3. Divide the class into two groups and have the groups sit single file facing forward.
4. Place the deck of noun and verb cards facedown between the first students in each line.
5. Place a noun and a verb container several feet in front of each group.

Object of the game:

to correctly identify more words as nouns or verbs

Verbs	
did	marry
forget	ran
get	see
give	sing
go	sit
grow	speak
hear	start
knew	teach

Nouns	
boy	kitchen
car	path
city	porch
chair	puppy
church	river
dime	street
apple	teacher
king	zoo

Playing the game:

1. At the teacher's signal, the first student in each team lineup takes a card from the deck, reads it silently, and then passes it to the teammate behind her.
2. Each team member silently reads the card and then passes it on.
3. The last team member in line walks quickly to the containers, drops the card into the appropriate one, and then takes his place at the front of his team's line.
4. Play continues in this manner until each student has had a turn putting a card in the container.
5. The teacher checks the words in each container. The team with more correctly placed cards wins.

©The Education Center, Inc.

Digging Deep for Adjectives

Skill: using adjectives

Number of players: whole class

Materials:

- 3–5 classroom objects for the whole class
- sheet of paper for each group
- pencil for each group
- clock or timer for the whole class

Teacher preparation:

1. Choose three to five classroom objects for students to describe and place them out of sight.
2. Divide students into equal groups of three to five.
3. Designate a writer and a reader in each group.
4. Explain to students that they must pretend that 2,000 years have passed. They are scientists who have discovered ancient objects buried deep in the ruins of an old classroom. Each group's task is to list adjectives describing the strange, ancient objects.

Object of the game:

to list the greatest number of unique adjectives describing classroom objects

Playing the game:

1. The teacher brings an object out from its hidden location. Each group has two minutes to list as many adjectives as possible to describe the object.
2. The teacher calls on one group to begin. The reader from that group reads each adjective on the group's list. If another group has the same adjective, the reader from that group says, "Dig deeper!" The adjective is then crossed off every list where it appears.
3. Each remaining group shares its list of adjectives and crosses off any adjectives listed by another group.
4. Then each group counts the adjectives left on its list. The winner of the round is the group with the most remaining adjectives.
5. Assign new group readers and writers and play again with another object. Continue playing as time allows. The winner is the group with the greatest total number of unique adjectives.

©The Education Center, Inc.

Variation:

Have students list verbs describing what can be appropriately done with particular objects. For example, a book can be read, opened, closed, put, bought, etc.

Assorted Adjectives

Skill: using adjectives

Number of players: 2–6

Materials:

- copy of page 46 for each player
- 9 prepared squares for each group
- small container for each group
- 1-minute timer for each group

Teacher preparation:

1. Make nine two-inch tagboard squares. Write each of these letters on a different square: *S, T, R, M, L, H, D, A,* and *W.*
2. Put the letters in a small container.
3. Remind students that an adjective describes a noun by telling how many, which one, or what kind.

Object of the game:

to earn the most points for using unique adjectives beginning with specific letters

Playing the game:

1. One player draws a letter from the container. Each player writes the letter in the top box of the first column on her paper.
2. A player starts the one-minute timer. Players describe each of the nouns on the left using an adjective that begins with the chosen letter. Each player tries to be original. If a player cannot think of an adjective for one of the nouns, she leaves that space blank.
3. When time is up, one player reads the noun. Then each player, in turn, reads the adjective she has written for that noun. If only one player used an adjective, and all other players agree that it describes the noun, then that player earns a point.
4. Tally points at the bottom of the column.
5. A player draws a new letter and then the players play again, using the second column.
6. After four rounds, the player with the most points wins.

©The Education Center, Inc.

Assorted Adjectives

letter			
yourself			
your school			
an airplane			
your playground			
a car			
your teacher			
a dog			
a sandwich			
your desk			
your family			
Points earned:			

Total points:

A Picture's Worth a Thousand Adjectives

Skill: using adjectives

Number of players: 10 or more

Materials for each group:

- 10 prepared picture cards
- chalk and chalkboard

Teacher preparation:

1. Cut ten large pictures of objects from magazines.
2. Glue each picture onto a 9" x 12" sheet of construction paper.
3. Divide students into two even teams.
4. Label one end of the board "Team 1" and the other end "Team 2."
5. Display a picture card on the middle of the chalkboard.

Object of the game:

to earn team points by listing more adjectives to describe a picture

Playing the game:

1. The first player from Team 1 goes to the board and writes an adjective that describes the object in the picture. Limit answer time to 15 seconds.
2. The first player on Team 2 writes a different adjective.
3. Team 1's next player adds an adjective to his team's list. Players and teams continue taking turns until one team cannot list another adjective within the time limit. Then play passes to the other team for one last word before the round ends.
4. The team that lists more adjectives wins the round. In the event of a tie, each team receives a point.
5. Display a new picture and continue play as time allows.

Variation:

Write one element above the picture that students may not describe, such as the object's color, size, or shape.

Adverb Treasure Trail

Skill: identifying adverbs

Number of players: 2

Materials:
- copy of the gameboard on page 49 for each player
- crayon for each player
- 20 prepared index cards for each pair
- envelope for each pair

Teacher preparation:
1. Program the front of each index card with a sentence from the list on page 49. (Don't underline the adverb.) Write the adverb (underlined word) in pencil on the back.
2. Put the cards in an envelope so that neither the sentences nor the answers can be seen.

Object of the game:

to correctly identify the adverbs in given sentences and be the first player to color all the footprints on the Adverb Treasure Trail

Playing the game:
1. Player 1 takes a card from the envelope and holds it up so Player 2 can read the sentence.
2. Player 2 reads the sentence and picks out the adverb. Player 1 checks Player 2's answer by referring to the back of the card.
3. If Player 2 correctly picks the adverb, she colors a footprint on the Treasure Trail and sets the card aside. If she does not find the adverb, the card is put back into the envelope.
4. Player 2 takes a card from the envelope, and Player 1 takes a turn.
5. Players take turns in this manner until one player colors all the footprints, reaches the treasure, and wins the game.

©The Education Center, Inc.

Variation:

Cut out life-size footprints and create a treasure trail around your classroom. Divide students into two teams and play as directed above, except with a treasure hunter for each team who moves along the trail as correct answers are given. Provide an appropriate treasure for the team that reaches the end of the trail first.

Adverb Treasure Trail

1. Sam walked <u>softly</u> down the beach.
2. Erin <u>quickly</u> spied a shiny object.
3. A parrot flew <u>straight</u> to Tom's head.
4. Water <u>lightly</u> rocked the boat.
5. A fish jumped <u>up</u>.
6. The fish landed <u>noisily</u> in the boat.
7. Ted <u>slowly</u> counted six shells.
8. Erin sails <u>daily</u>.
9. Who <u>secretly</u> found the treasure?
10. Ken ran <u>fast</u>.
11. He <u>nearly</u> saw the coins and jewels.
12. This sand <u>gently</u> tickles my feet.
13. Does Joel know the boat tipped <u>over</u>?
14. The clam dug <u>deep</u>.
15. Can fish swim <u>backward</u>?
16. Who <u>correctly</u> counted the coins?
17. Jenny <u>roughly</u> drew a map.
18. Nate <u>finally</u> found the boat.
19. <u>Calmly</u> bring the boat to the shore.
20. Anita shouted <u>loudly</u>, "I found it!"

Fishing for Adverbs

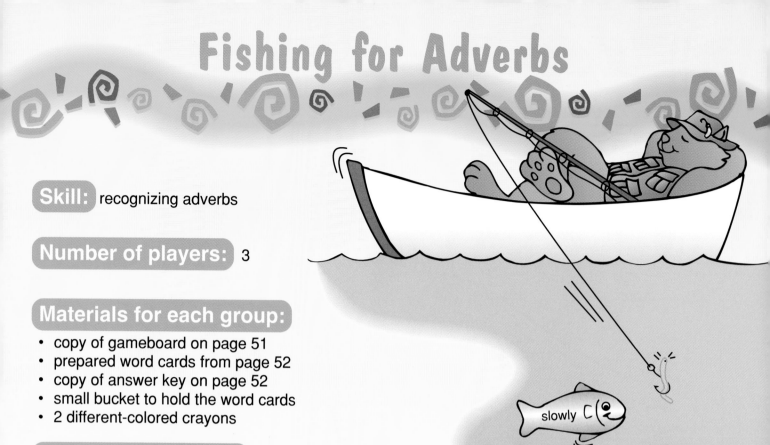

Skill: recognizing adverbs

Number of players: 3

Materials for each group:
- copy of gameboard on page 51
- prepared word cards from page 52
- copy of answer key on page 52
- small bucket to hold the word cards
- 2 different-colored crayons

Teacher preparation:
1. Cut apart the word cards and put them in the bucket.
2. Give the answer key to Player 3.

Object of the game:

to be the first player to identify three adverbs for each category on the gameboard

Playing the game:
1. Players 1 and 2 play the game. Player 3 checks the answers against the key.
2. Player 1 chooses a word card from the bucket and reads it aloud. He decides whether the word is an adverb. If it is an adverb, he decides whether the adverb tells how, when, or where. He reports his answer to the key checker, who tells him whether he is correct. If Player 1 is correct, he colors a fish in the matching category. If the word is not an adverb or if he gives an incorrect answer, his turn ends. The card is set aside.
3. Player 2 takes a turn. Play continues in this manner.
4. If a player has already colored three fish in one category and draws another adverb for that category, he returns the card to the bucket and loses his turn. A player also loses a turn if he draws a card that reads "The fish got away!"
5. The first player to color three fish in each category is the winner.

©The Education Center, Inc.

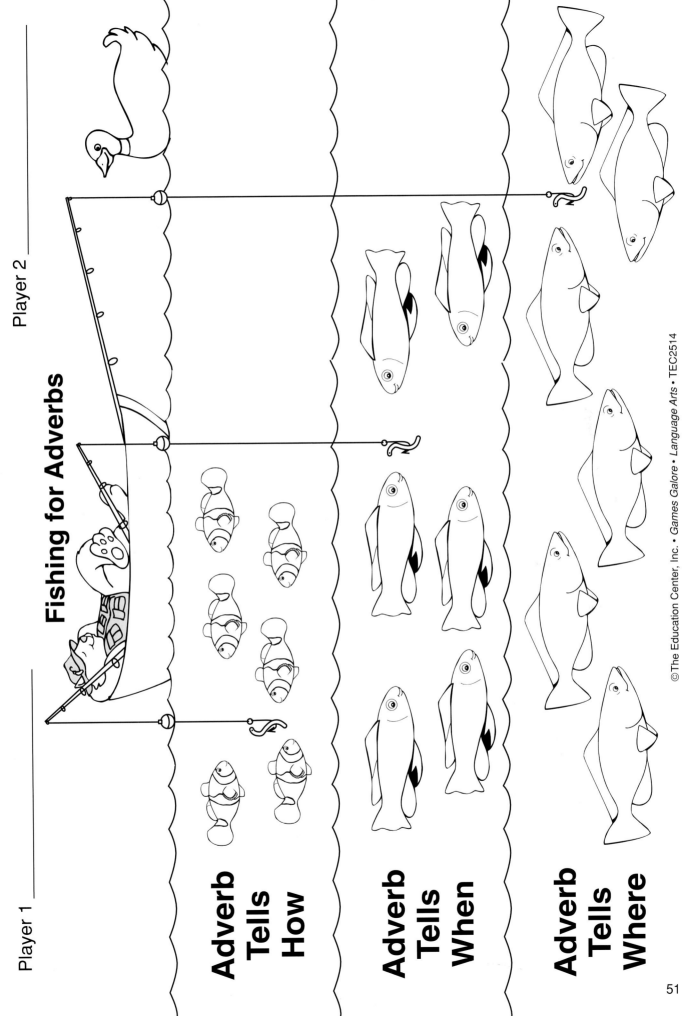

Player 1

Player 2

Fishing for Adverbs

Adverb Tells How

Adverb Tells When

Adverb Tells Where

louder	quietly	badly	slowly	softly
happily	quickly	faster	The fish got away!	blue
before	today	early	never	finally
often	now	soon	The fish got away!	dinner
inside	near	up	here	down
under	away	above	The fish got away!	four

Answer Key		
Adverbs Telling How	**Adverbs Telling When**	**Adverbs Telling Where**
badly quickly	before now	above inside
faster quietly	early often	away near
happily slowly	finally soon	down under
louder softly	never today	here up

Fiddle-Dee-Dee, We Agree!

Skill: identifying subject and verb agreement

Number of players: 2

Materials for each pair:
- copy of the gameboard on page 54
- prepared sentence strips in a small paper bag
- 2 different-colored crayons
- copy of the answer key on page 95

Teacher preparation:
1. Cut apart the gameboard and a copy of the sentence strips on page 54.
2. Store the sentence strips in the bag.

Object of the game:

to be the player who correctly makes more subject and verb agreements and colors more musical notes

Playing the game:

1. Each player chooses one crayons.
2. Player 1 pulls a sentence strip from the bag and reads it aloud, completing the sentence with the appropriate verb.
3. Player 2 refers to the answer key to confirm Player 1's answer. If the answer is correct, Player 1 colors a corresponding musical note on the gameboard and then her turn is over. If the answer is incorrect, Player 1's turn is over. Player 1 sets the sentence strip aside.
4. Players take turns until all of the musical notes are colored or until no more matches can be made. The player who colors more musical notes wins.

©The Education Center, Inc.

Variation:

Create new sentence strips and have students identify pronouns or adverbs.

Fiddle-Dee-Dee, We Agree!

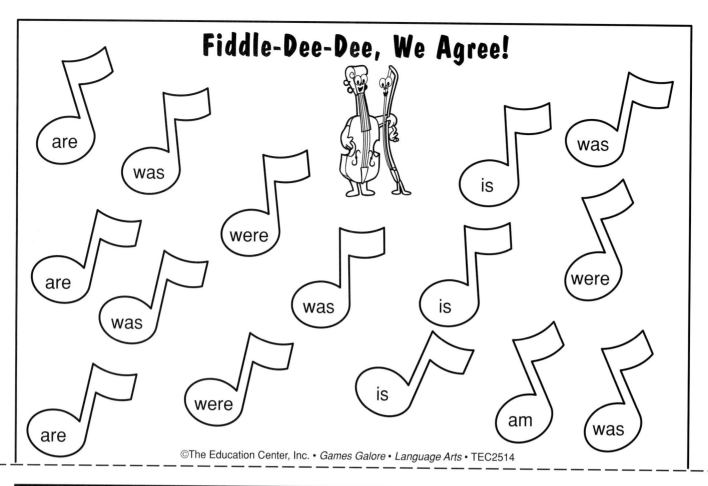

1. I ___ wearing a green shirt today.	11. ___ you feeling well right now?
2. Yesterday I ___ watching TV.	12. ___ you in the library yesterday?
3. He ___ doing his homework now.	13. The teacher ___ baking a cake now.
4. She ___ at school yesterday.	14. The teacher ___ wearing pink yesterday.
5. Now they ___ late.	15. Who ___ walking to school now?
6. They ___ playing football last night.	16. Who ___ in the gym yesterday?
7. We ___ eating cookies now.	17. ___ Bill the captain now?
8. We ___ in the mall last week.	18. ___ Sue checking out a book yesterday?
9. Nine girls ___ eating lunch now.	19. The hamster ___ in his cage now.
10. Nine boys ___ wearing sweaters.	20. The hamster ___ here yesterday.

All About Adjectives

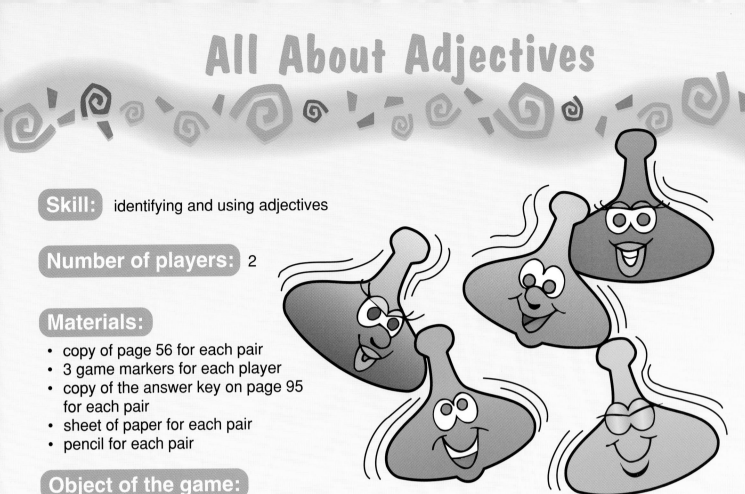

Skill: identifying and using adjectives

Number of players: 2

Materials:

- copy of page 56 for each pair
- 3 game markers for each player
- copy of the answer key on page 95 for each pair
- sheet of paper for each pair
- pencil for each pair

Object of the game:

to be the first player to move all of his game pieces into his opponent's home base

Playing the game:

1. Each player puts a game marker in each box in his home base.
2. Player 1 moves one of his game markers vertically, horizontally, or diagonally one space into a free box. Players may not move backwards.
3. Player 1 reads aloud the sentence in the box he lands in. He chooses the adjective that completes the sentence.
4. Player 2 refers to the answer key to confirm the answer. If Player 1 is incorrect, he moves his game marker back to his home base.
5. Players continue taking turns until one player moves all three game markers into the other's home base.

©The Education Center, Inc.

1. I ate a _____ apple.

crisp talk pear

2. The car drove on the _____ road.

candy bumpy drink

3. The _____ friends played together.

smile peek three

4. The kitten sat in the _____ basket.

brown girl draws

5. She ate her _____ soup.

type book salty

6. The artist drew a _____ picture.

crayon colorful up

7. The _____ rocket flew to the moon.

made tall fish

8. I am under the _____ blanket.

blue cup lake

9. The _____ book was on the table.

sing ice thick

10. Those _____ fish are swimming.

web four ate

11. She walked near the _____ car.

water shiny cut

12. The _____ dog caught the ball.

large box grow

13. The _____ garden needs weeding.

sits big note

14. The cowboy rode on his _____ horse.

card pine spotted

15. The _____ fire burned brightly.

hot blows mile

16. He ran to the _____ house.

hair green swims

17. The _____ polar bear growled.

wood friends unhappy

18. The plane flew through the _____ clouds.

number fluffy globe

19. The _____ king has a crown.

jolly saves file

20. We hear a _____ whistle.

flag day loud

Player 2 Home

Punctuation Zoo!

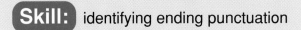

Skill: identifying ending punctuation

Number of players: whole class

Materials for the whole class:
- pocket chart
- 3 prepared index cards
- copy of pages 58 and 59
- chalkboard or chart paper
- chalk or marker

Teacher preparation:
1. Prominently display the pocket chart.
2. Write a different punctuation mark (., ?, !) on three index cards and display each on a middle row of the chart.
3. Cut apart the sentence cards. Then stack and display them below the middle row with the sentences facing the chart.
4. Keep the answer key card for use during the game.
5. Divide the class into two seated teams. Write "Team 1" and "Team 2" on the chalkboard or chart paper.

Object of the game:

to be the team to punctuate more sentences correctly

Playing the game:
1. The first player from Team 1 draws a sentence card from the chart, reads it aloud, and states its correct ending punctuation mark. The teacher checks the key.
2. If correct, the player writes a tally mark below his team's name. If incorrect, the next player on the opposing team tries to answer correctly to receive a bonus point. Even if the player misses the bonus point, he takes his turn. The sentence card is placed on the chart near its matching punctuation mark.
3. Play alternates between teams until all of the sentences have been used. The team with more points wins the game.

1. The parrot ate a nut	9. Meet me by the monkey cage
2. This zoo has zebras	10. How many animals live in this zoo
3. Why can't I see the zebras	11. When will the baby bear be born
4. Wait You're going the wrong way	12. The park closes at 6:00
5. Will you come with me to see the snakes	13. There are two gift shops near the exit
6. Tigers have stripes	14. Don't stand near that puddle
7. That elephant is huge	15. Take your food wrapper to the trash can
8. Try not to wake the raccoons	6. My favorite animal is the lion

17. Sam, watch out

18. Why do turtles move so slowly

19. Hurry The show is starting now

20. Do you want to feed the bunnies

21. What kind of fish is that

22. Where would I find the tropical birds

23. I think this zoo is great

24. The zookeeper is feeding fish to the bear

25. What did you do at the zoo all day

26. Write a story about your trip to the zoo

27. Let's go see the kangaroo

28. Have you ever seen a monkey swing by its tail

29. We will take a train ride to see all of the animals

30. Monkeys are different from gorillas

Answer Key

1. .	9. .	17. !	25. ?
2. .	10. ?	18. ?	26. .
3. ?	11. ?	19. !	27. .
4. !	12. .	20. ?	28. ?
5. ?	13. .	21. ?	29. .
6. .	14. .	22. ?	30. .
7. !	15. .	23. !	
8. .	16. .	24. .	

Capitalization Scavenger Hunt

Skill: locating capitalized words

Number of players: whole class (divided into groups of 3–5)

Materials:
- discarded magazines for each group
- discarded newspapers for each group
- sheet of chart paper for each group
- scissors for each player
- glue for each player

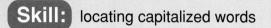

Teacher preparation:
1. On the chalkboard, write the following scavenger hunt items:
   - 4 proper names
   - 4 street names
   - 4 abbreviated titles, such as *Mrs., Dr., Mr.*
   - 4 city names
2. Divide students into groups of 3–5.

Object of the game:

to be the first group to correctly complete the capitalization scavenger hunt

Playing the game:
1. At the teacher's signal, each group member searches a magazine or newspaper section for an item on the scavenger hunt list.
2. She cuts out the item and then glues it onto her group's chart paper. Then she looks for another item on the list.
3. The first group to find everything on the list and complete its chart wins.

Variation:

For a two-player game, have players search textbooks for capitalized items of your choice. When a player finds an example, she writes the word or words on notebook paper. If desired, have her list the page number where the example was found. The winner is the player who finds more correct examples in a specified amount of time.

Tap It

Skill: identifying correct capitalization

Number of players: 2

Materials for each pair:
- 17 prepared index cards
- envelope

Teacher preparation:
1. On each of 16 index cards, write a different word (11 that are usually capitalized and five that are not) using lowercase letters. Label each card with a number 1–16.
2. On the remaining card, write each number and the corresponding word with the correct capitalization. Label the card "Answer Key" and place it in an envelope.

Object of the game:
to be the player to tap and collect more cards

Playing the game:
1. A player shuffles the cards and then lays them facedown in a stack between the players.
2. Player 1 turns over the top card and lays it on the playing surface.
3. If the word needs a capital letter, each player races to cover the card with his hand (to tap it).
4. The player who taps it checks the key. If he's correct, he keeps the card. If the player is incorrect, he places the card at the bottom of the stack.
5. If the card does not need a capital letter it is moved to the side.
6. Player 2 then turns a card over to continue play. Players take turns until all of the cards have been used. The player who collects more cards wins.

Variation:

Program the cards using a mixture of base words with correct and incorrect prefixes or suffixes. Players identify whether the base word and prefix or suffix shown make sense.

Catching Capitals

Skill: identifying needed capitalization

Number of players: 2

Materials for each pair:
- copy of page 63
- 2 pencils

Object of the game:
to be the player to correct, initial, and claim more boxes

Playing the game:
1. Each player writes her name at the top of the gameboard.
2. Player 1 draws a line vertically or horizontally to connect two dots on the gameboard.
3. Play alternates until a player draws a line to enclose a box.
4. That player reads the sentence aloud and points out the word(s) that should be capitalized.
5. If the player is correct, she claims the box by writing her initials inside. Then she takes another turn. If she is incorrect, her opponent can claim the box by pointing out the words.
6. Players take turns until all of the boxes have been claimed. The player who claims more boxes wins.

Variation:

Add a punctuation challenge! White-out the ending punctuation for each sentence. To claim the box, each player must identify the capital letter needed as well as the correct ending punctuation.

Player 1 _____   Player 2 _____

Mr. jones is my teacher.

Today is tuesday.

Let's play at keller park.

Is your birthday in june?

my sister and I like to read!

My snail's name is speedy.

you are my best friend!

She goes to lincoln School.

kelly, do you like to play ball?

Turn right on lambert Road.

We ate at jake's.

Who will go to the zoo on friday?

My dog's name is rover.

I will visit dr. Taylor in October.

Let's go to Wonderful water World!

Mother's Day is in may.

do you like to eat spinach?

I have a book titled *bugs and Bears.*

yesterday was Monday.

Meet me at pine street.

Spell 'n' Toss

Skill: spelling

Number of players: whole class

Materials for the class:
- list of 25 spelling words
- masking tape
- 3 plastic containers
- beanbag

Teacher preparation:
1. Put a strip of masking tape on the floor as a standing line.
2. Label the containers "1 Point," "2 Points," and "3 Points."
3. Beginning with the one-point container, set the three containers, one behind the other, at equal intervals within tossing distance of the line.
4. Divide the class into two teams. Have each team sit in a line on the floor facing the chalkboard.
5. Write "Team 1" and "Team 2" on the chalkboard.

Object of the game:
to earn more points by spelling words correctly and tossing a beanbag

Playing the game:
1. A player from Team 1 stands behind the line facing the containers.
2. The teacher calls out a spelling word from the list and then the player spells the word aloud.
3. The opposing team signals thumbs-up for a correct spelling or thumbs-down for an incorrect spelling.
4. If the teacher says the spelling is correct, the player tosses a beanbag into one of the containers. Then the player records the corresponding number of tally marks below her team's name. (She tosses until the beanbag lands in a container.) If the spelling is incorrect, the player's turn ends.
5. Teams take turns until each student has had a chance to spell. The team with more points at the end of the game wins.

©The Education Center, Inc.

Variation:
Use words with prefixes and suffixes instead of spelling words. Each player correctly states the prefix or suffix and then tosses the beanbag.

Spelling Bees

Skill: spelling

Number of players: 4

Materials for each group:

- list of 20 spelling words
- 20 prepared cards
- sheet of paper
- pencil

Teacher preparation:

1. Cut each index card in half.
2. Write a spelling word on each half.

Object of the game:

to be the player who correctly spells the most words and has the most points at the end of the game

Playing the game:

1. Shuffle the cards. Lay them facedown in a stack on the playing surface.
2. To keep score, write each player's name on a sheet of paper. Give each player 10 points to start the game.
3. Player 1 is the reader and scorekeeper during the first round. He draws a card from the stack and reads aloud the word shown.
4. The player on his left (Player 2) repeats the word, spells it, and says "Buzz" when he is finished. Player 1 checks the spelling by looking at the card and gives Player 2 one point if the spelling is correct.
5. If either of the other two players disagrees with the spelling, she says "Sting." Then she spells the word. If she is correct, she earns one point and Player 2 does not. If the player who says "Sting" spells the word incorrectly, or if the word was already spelled correctly, she loses a point.
6. If no player challenges the spelling and Player 1 finds that it is incorrect, no player earns a point.
7. Players take turns until all of the words have been spelled. The player with the most points at the end of the game wins.

"Un-bee-lievable" Spelling!

Skill: spelling

Number of players: whole class

Materials for the class:
- 2 copies of page 67
- chalkboard

Teacher preparation:
1. Color and laminate the copies of page 67. Then cut out each bee's body parts.
2. Divide the class into two teams.
3. On the chalkboard, write "Team 1" and "Team 2."
4. Randomly tape one set of bee body pieces near, but not below, each team's name.

Object of the game:

to be the first team to earn three points by assembling its spelling bee

Playing the game:
1. A player from Team 1 walks to the board and then faces the class.
2. The teacher says a spelling word. The student says the word aloud, spells it, and then says it again.
3. If the spelling is correct, the student places one bee body part under her team's name. If the spelling is incorrect, no bee body part is moved.
4. Players continue taking turns as each team tries to earn all of its bee body parts.
5. When a team completes a bee, a point is marked near the team's name and that team's bee parts are scattered again.
6. Play continues until a team earns three points.

©The Education Center, Inc.

Variation:

Play with a group of three students. For two students, provide a sheet of paper, a copy of page 67 (uncut), and a pencil. Provide one spelling list for the group. Designate one student to call out each word from the list to be spelled. Players 1 and 2 play as above, except that with each correct spelling, a player draws a bee part on her paper and crosses it off on her copy of page 67. The first player to complete her bee wins.

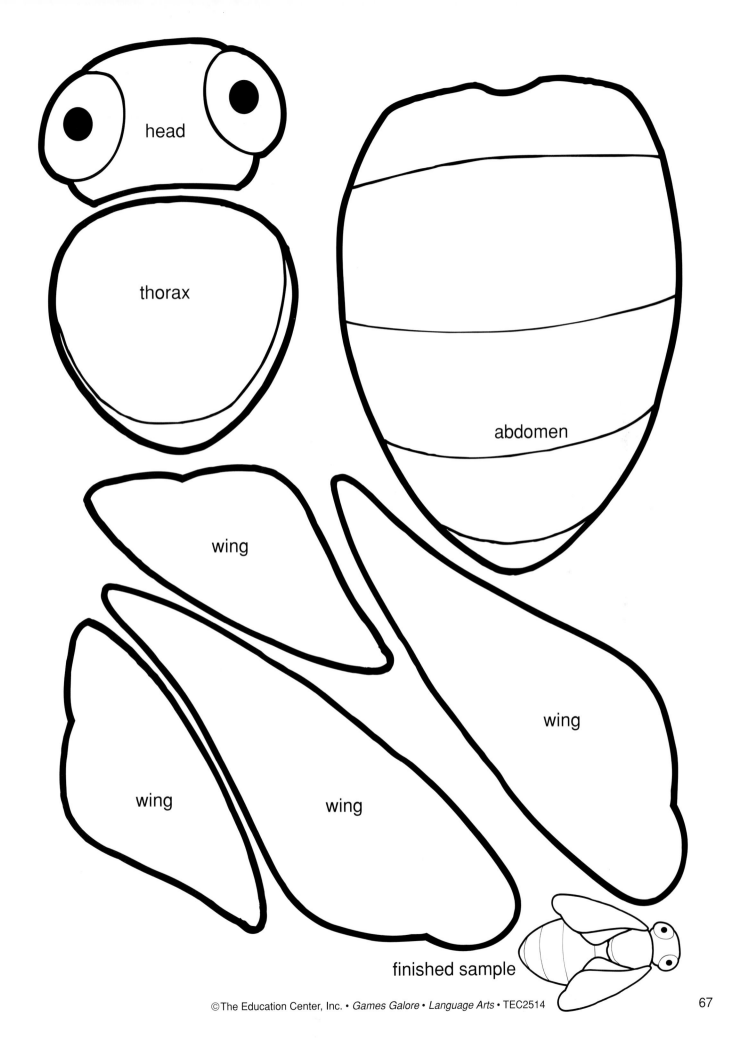

head

thorax

abdomen

wing

wing

wing

wing

wing

finished sample

Compound-Word Climb

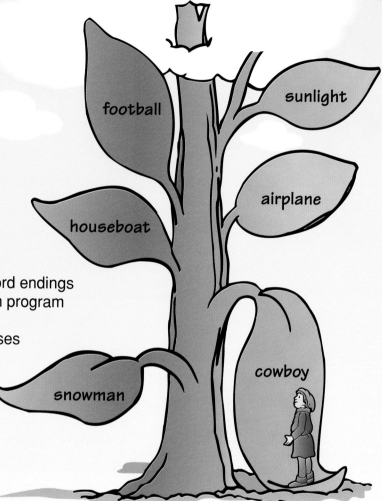

Skill: making compound words

Number of players: 2–4

Materials:
- copy of page 69 for each player
- 4 prepared dice for each group
- pencil for each player

Teacher preparation:
1. Make four copies of page 17 (mask out word endings before copying). Cut out each die and then program as follows:
   - Die 1: foot, house, door, cow, man, glasses
   - Die 2: basket, air, night, box, bell, snow
   - Die 3: way, stalk, ball, port, knob, light
   - Die 4: boy, shoe, bean, plane, star, sun
2. Assemble each die.

Object of the game:
to be the first player to reach the top of the beanstalk by correctly labeling each leaf with a compound word

Playing the game:
1. Player 1 rolls all four dice to show four words.
2. She reads aloud each word and tries to make at least one compound word by combining two of the words shown.
3. Starting at the bottom of the "Compound-Word Climb" page, she writes each compound word on a beanstalk leaf. If she cannot make a word, her turn ends.
4. Players take turns until one reaches the top of her beanstalk.

©The Education Center, Inc.

Compound-Word Climb

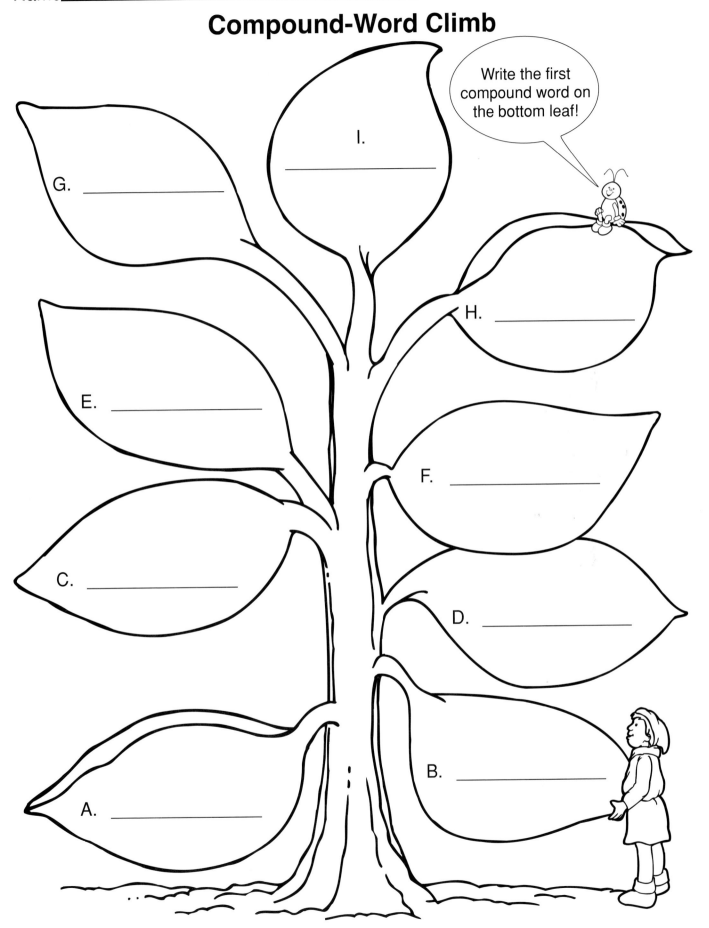

Write the first compound word on the bottom leaf!

I. _____

G. _____

H. _____

E. _____

F. _____

C. _____

D. _____

A. _____

B. _____

"Egg-ceptional" Compound-Word Search

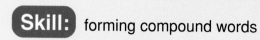

Skill: forming compound words

Number of players: 2–3

Materials:

- 6 plastic, snap-together eggs for each player
- half an empty egg carton for each player
- permanent marker

Teacher preparation:

1. Write a compound word in permanent marker on each egg (half on each side as shown).
2. Pull the eggs apart and hide half of each egg in a designated playing area.
3. Give six of the remaining egg halves in an egg carton half to each player.

Object of the game:

to be the first player to collect six compound words

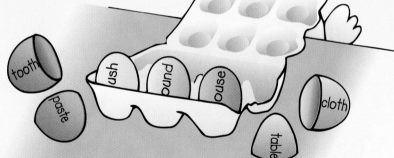

Playing the game:

1. At the teacher's signal, each player reads the word on each egg half in his carton.
2. Each player looks for a word match for each egg half. (A correct match is a compound word that makes sense and has both egg halves the same color.)
3. After finding all six compound words, the player gives the egg carton to the teacher to check.
4. For each incorrect match, the teacher will hide the egg halves again. Players with incorrect matches continue their search.

Variation:

Write synonyms, homophones, or antonyms on the eggs.

Compound Caterpillar

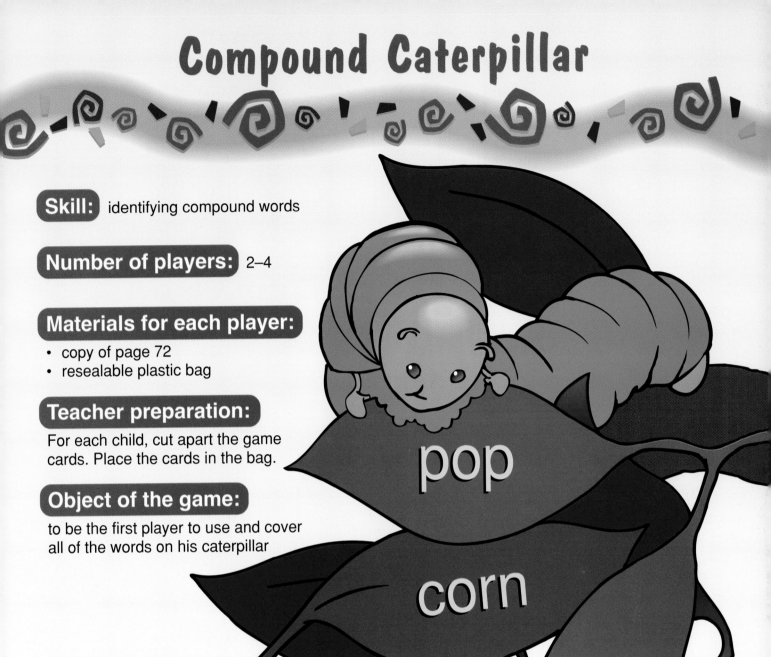

Skill: identifying compound words

Number of players: 2–4

Materials for each player:
- copy of page 72
- resealable plastic bag

Teacher preparation:
For each child, cut apart the game cards. Place the cards in the bag.

Object of the game:
to be the first player to use and cover all of the words on his caterpillar

pop

corn

Playing the game:
1. Each player shuffles and stacks his game cards.
2. Player 1 draws three cards and reads the word aloud. Then he reads the first word on his gameboard aloud, and determines if one of the words on his cards makes a compound word with the gameboard word.
3. If a compound word is made, the player lays the card on the matching space on the caterpillar. He puts the other two cards on the bottom of the card stack. If a compound word is not made, the player puts all the cards at the bottom of his stack.
4. Players alternate turns. During each turn, a player uses his next uncovered word on the caterpillar.
5. The first player to cover all of his caterpillar's words wins.

Variation:
Play the game using game cards with prefixes or suffixes and gameboards that show corresponding base words.

your	sun	swim	tug	air	cup
sea	hair	play	fire	after	foot

Compound Caterpillars

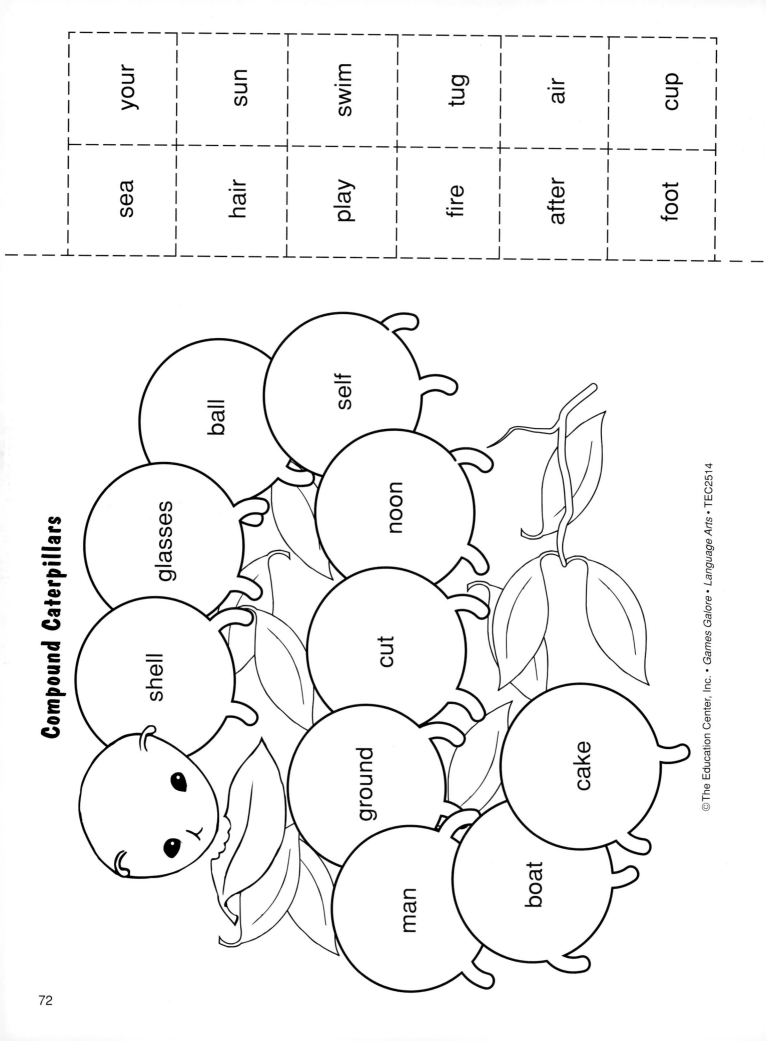

ball

self

glasses

noon

shell

cut

ground

cake

man

boat

Word Builder

Skill: forming compound words

Number of players: 2

Materials for each pair:
- copy of gameboards and game cards on page 74
- 2 crayons

Teacher preparation:
Cut apart the gameboards and game cards on page 74.

Object of the game:
to be the first builder to color all of the bricks on his gameboard

Playing the game:
1. A player (builder) shuffles and stacks the game cards facedown on the playing surface.
2. Builder 1 draws a card and reads the word aloud. He studies his gameboard to see whether one of the words on it can be paired with the word on the card to make a compound word.
3. If a compound word can be made, the builder colors the corresponding brick on the gameboard and sets the card aside. If a compound word cannot be made, the builder puts the card at the bottom of the card stack.
4. Players take turns until one builder colors each brick on his gameboard and wins the game.

©The Education Center, Inc.

chalk	pan	bean	fire	sea	pop
horse	fish	mail	desk	clean	note
air	down	gum	cow	side	foot
name	home	book	finger	wind	clothes

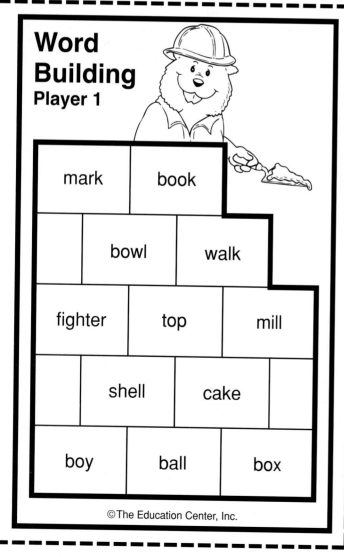

Word Building
Player 1

mark	book	
	bowl	walk
fighter	top	mill
	shell	cake
boy	ball	box

©The Education Center, Inc.

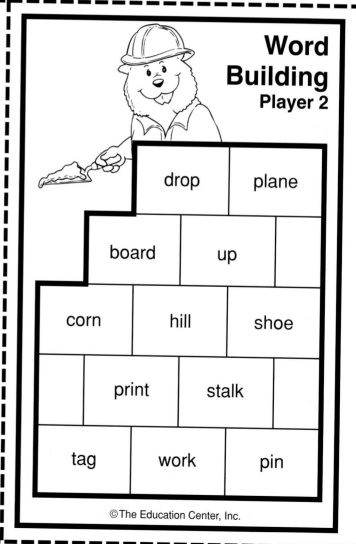

Word Building
Player 2

	drop	plane
board	up	
corn	hill	shoe
	print	stalk
tag	work	pin

©The Education Center, Inc.

Navigating Prefixes

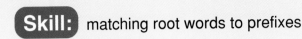

Skill: matching root words to prefixes

Number of players: 2

Materials:

- laminated sailing scene gameboard for each player
- sailboat on page 76 for each player
- copy of the prefix cards on page 76 for each pair
- copy of the boat hull cards on page 76 for each pair
- wipe-off marker for each player
- facial tissue for each player
- dictionary

Teacher preparation:

1. Draw and color two 6" x 18" sailing scene game-boards—each with five lines and numbers as shown. Laminate.
2. Color the sailboats if desired; then cut them out.
3. Cut out the prefix and boat hull cards.

Object of the game:

to pair root words and prefixes to make words that match the definitions on the boat hulls

Playing the game:

1. Place the boat hull cards facedown in a stack and spread out the prefix cards faceup between the players.
2. Each player places her sailboat near the first line on her gameboard.
3. Player 1 draws a boat hull card and places it on her sailboat.
4. She writes the root word (underlined in the definition) on the first line on her gameboard.
5. She reads the definition on the hull card. She chooses the prefix card.
6. Player 2 refers to the dictionary to check the answer. If it is correct, Player 1 returns the prefix card to the table, sets the boat hull aside, and moves her boat to the next line on her gameboard.
7. If her answer is incorrect, she returns the prefix card to the table, places the hull on the bottom of the draw pile, and wipes the root word off her gameboard. She does not move her boat.
8. Players take turns until one fills in all five lines and wins the game.

©The Education Center, Inc.

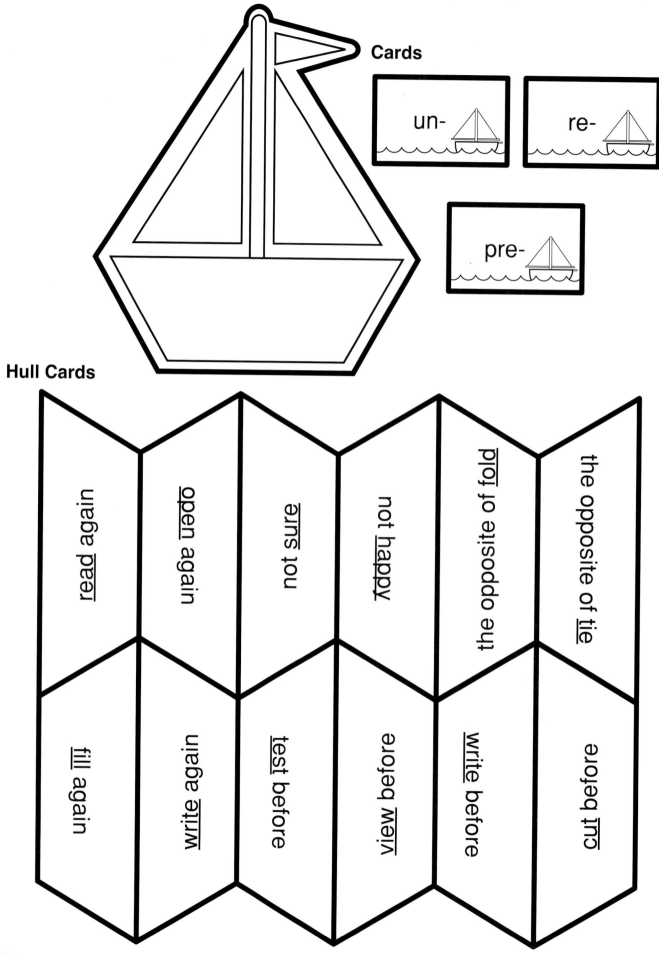

Cards

un-

re-

pre-

Hull Cards

read again

open again

not sure

not happy

the opposite of fold

the opposite of tie

fill again

write again

test before

view before

write before

cut before

Prefix Pizza

Skill: identifying prefixes

Number of players: 2

Materials for each pair:
- copy of page 78
- copy of page 79
- resealable plastic bag
- dictionary

Teacher preparation:

Cut apart the game cards. Store them in the bag.

Object of the game:

to be the first player to correctly place all of her toppings on her pizza half

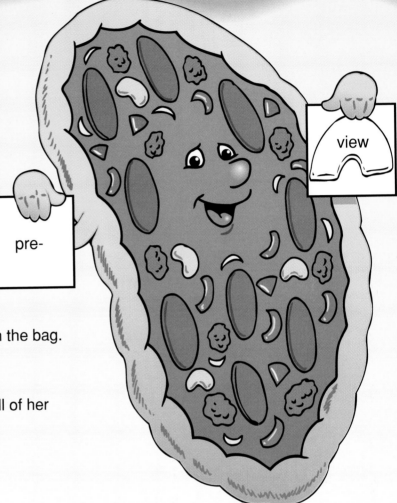

Playing the game:
1. A player shuffles the game cards and then lays them facedown in a stack on the playing surface.
2. Player 1 draws a card and reads aloud the word shown. (If she draws a "Lose a turn" card, Player 2 takes a turn.)
3. The player looks for a prefix on her gameboard half that will make a word when paired with the word card.
4. If she can make a word, she lays the topping on the corresponding pizza space. Students may check words in the dictionary as needed. If she cannot make a word, she puts the card at the bottom of the card stack.
5. Players take turns until one has correctly topped her pizza half.

Player 2

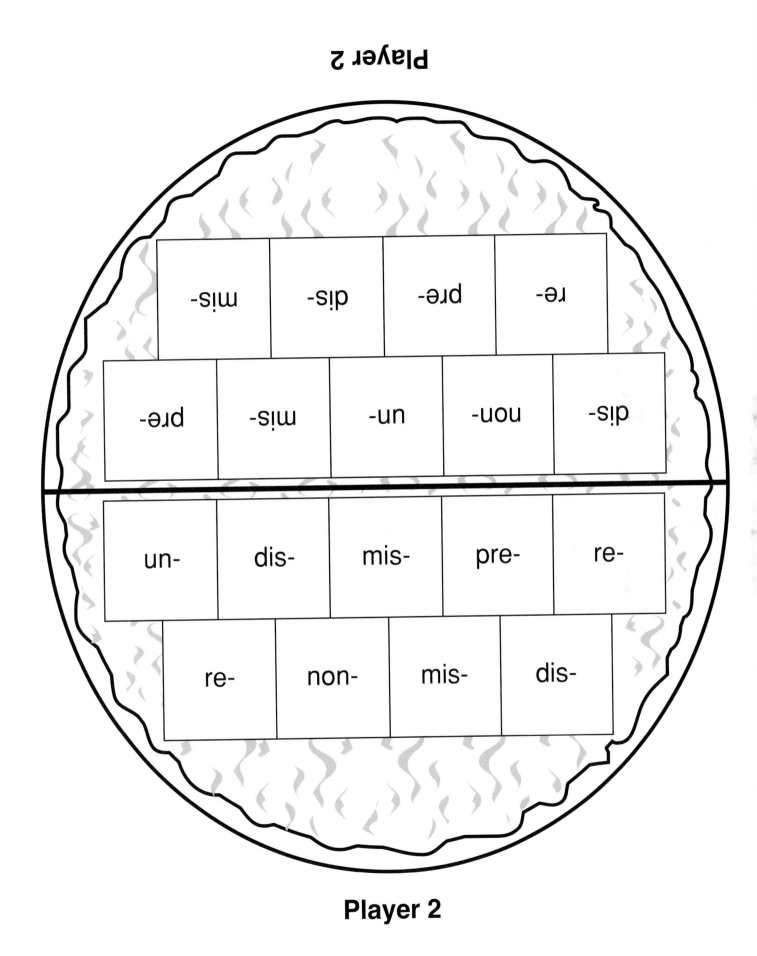

mis- dis- pre- re-

pre- mis- un- non- dis-

un- dis- mis- pre- re-

re- non- mis- dis-

Player 2

Scooping Up Suffixes

Skill: combining base words and suffixes to make new words

Number of players: 2

Materials for each pair:
- 30 prepared scoops for each pair
- 10 prepared cones for each pair
- copy of the answer key on page 81 in an envelope for each pair
- sheet of paper for each player
- pencil for each player

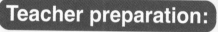

Teacher preparation:

1. Make five construction paper copies of the ice-cream scoops on page 81. Cut out each scoop.
2. Trim ten 2" x 3" brown construction paper rectangles into ice-cream cone shapes. Program each shape with one of the following base words: *hand, hope, like, love, mold, play, scare, spoon, true, wish.*
3. Place a copy of the key inside an envelope and then seal the envelope.

Object of the game:

to match more suffixes to base words

Playing the game:

1. Player 1 shuffles the ice-cream scoops and then stacks them facedown on the playing surface.
2. Player 2 deals five ice-cream cones to each player. Each player places his cones faceup on the playing surface.
3. Player 1 draws an ice-cream scoop. He reads the suffix on the scoop and then reads the word on each of his cones. He places the scoop on top of a cone with a word that can be combined with the suffix to make a new word. Then he writes the new word on his sheet of paper. If no word can be made, the scoop is set aside. A player may not use the same suffix more than one time on each cone.
4. Players continue taking turns until all of the scoops have been drawn.
5. Players open the envelope and compare their word lists with the answer key. Each player must cross off any word that is spelled incorrectly or is not listed on the key. The player with more correct words wins the game.

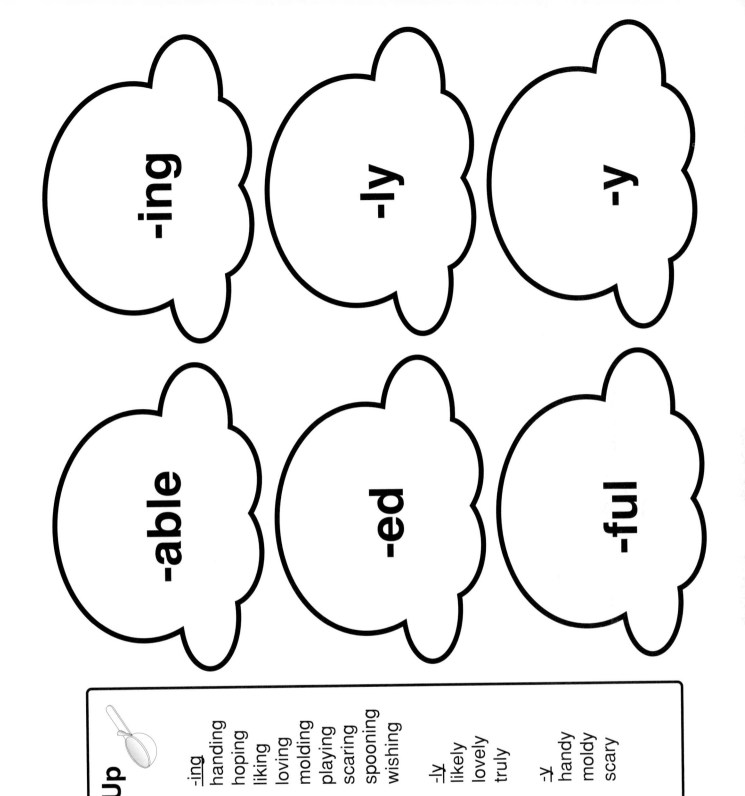

-ing

-ly

-y

-able

-ed

-ful

Scooping Up Suffixes

Key

-ing
handing
hoping
liking
loving
molding
playing
scaring
spooning
wishing

-ly
likely
lovely
truly

-y
handy
moldy
scary

-able
likable
lovable
moldable

-ed
handed
hoped
liked
loved
molded
played
scared
spooned
wished

-ful
handful
hopeful
playful
spoonful
wishful

Tennis Tally

Skill: adding suffixes

Number of players: 2

Materials for each pair:
- prepared game cards on page 83
- copy of the point card on page 83
- 2 pencils
- scrap paper
- dictionary

Teacher preparation:

Cut out the game cards.

Object of the game:

to earn more points by forming words with suffixes

Playing the game:

1. One player shuffles the playing cards and deals eight to each player. Each player places his deck of cards facedown on the playing surface.
2. Player 1 draws a card from his deck and reads it aloud. Then he repeatedly changes the word, adding each suffix from the point box to the end of the word.
3. When the addition of a suffix forms a word (even if it requires a spelling change such as beautiful), Player 1 receives the number of points shown on the point card under that suffix. When the addition of the suffix does not form a word, Player 1 receives no points. If players are unsure, they refer to a dictionary. Players draw tally marks on the scrap paper to keep score.
4. Players 1 and 2 take turns until all the cards have been read.
5. The winner is the player who earns the most points.

©The Education Center, Inc.

Tennis Tally

Point Card

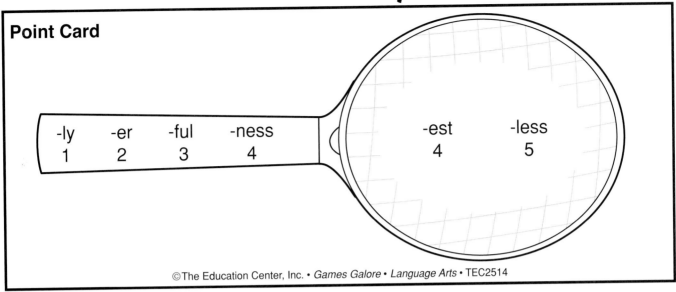

-ly	-er	-ful	-ness	-est	-less
1	2	3	4	4	5

Game Cards

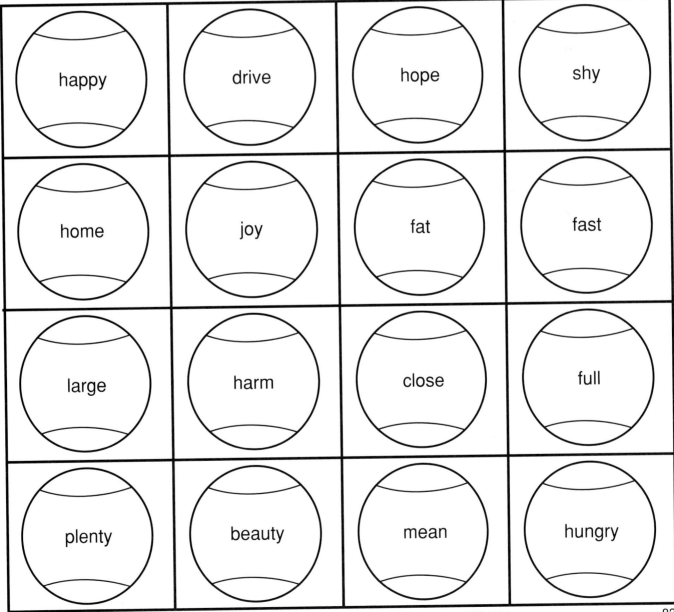

happy	drive	hope	shy
home	joy	fat	fast
large	harm	close	full
plenty	beauty	mean	hungry

Homophone Toss

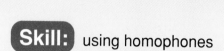

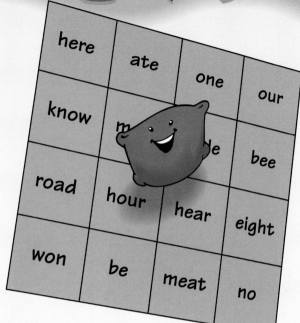

The grid shows: here, ate, one, our, know, m___, ___e, bee, road, hour, hear, eight, won, be, meat, no

Skill: using homophones

Number of players: 4

Materials for each group:

- prepared bulletin board paper
- beanbag
- dictionary
- masking tape

Teacher preparation:

1. Use a straightedge and marker to divide a 4' x 4' sheet of bulletin board paper into sixteen 1' x 1' squares.
2. Select eight homophone pairs. Write a different word in each square on the bulletin board paper.
3. Lay the paper on the floor. Then use tape to mark a toss line three feet from the paper's edge.
4. Divide students into two teams.

Object of the game:

to earn ten points by using homophones correctly in sentences

Playing the game:

1. Each team stands behind the toss line.
2. The first player on Team 1 throws the beanbag onto the programmed bulletin board paper. She reads the homophone on which the beanbag lands. She uses the word in a sentence. The other players agree with or reject the answer. They may check a dictionary. If the player gives a sentence that uses the homophone correctly, she earns a point for her team.
3. The first player on Team 2 takes a turn. Teams take turns until one earns ten points and wins the game.

©The Education Center, Inc.

Variation:

Prepare the bulletin board paper for a game to reinforce synonyms or antonyms. Select the word pairs, but write only one word from each pair on the paper. Play as above except that players name a synonym or antonym of the word the beanbag lands on. Points are earned for correct responses.

Seven Up for Synonyms

Skill: naming synonyms

Number of players: whole class

Materials:
- 50 prepared 1" x 2" paper strips
- container

Teacher preparation:
Program the paper strips with a variety of grade-appropriate words for which your students will give synonyms.

Object of the game:
to be one of the seven students standing at the end of the game

Playing the game:
1. The teacher chooses seven students to go to the front of the classroom.
2. The remaining students stay seated, put their heads on their desks, and close their eyes.
3. The seven standing students walk among their classmates. Each taps one child lightly on the shoulder and then silently returns to the front of the room.
4. When all of the original seven students have returned to the front of the room, they say, "Seven up for synonyms." All students lift their heads and open their eyes. The seven students who were tapped stand.
5. The teacher calls on each of the tapped students in turn, to choose a student who is standing at the front of the class. The chosen student draws a paper strip from the container and reads the word aloud. The tapped student gives a synonym for the word. If his response is correct, the students switch places.
6. Continue play as time allows.

©The Education Center, Inc.

Aunt Anym

Skill: pairing antonyms

Number of players: 2–3

Materials for each group:
- 31 prepared 3" x 5" index cards

Teacher preparation:
1. Generate a list of 15 antonyms, such as *empty* and *full, hot* and *cold.*
2. Write each antonym on a separate index card.
3. Cut a picture of a woman out of a discarded magazine. Tape the picture onto the remaining index card and then label it as shown.

Object of the game:
to pair antonym cards and be the first to discard all the cards in your hand

Playing the game:
1. Shuffle the cards and deal them to the players.
2. Player 1 begins by removing any antonym pairs she holds in her hand. All players must agree that the words are antonyms. Then the cards are set aside.
3. Player 1 takes a card from the player to her right. If the chosen card forms an antonym pair, the two cards are set aside.
4. Players 2 and 3 take a turn in the same manner.
5. When a player holds the Aunt Anym card, it is good strategy not to let the other players know.
6. The game is over when a player matches and discards all his cards. That player is declared the winner. The player who holds the Aunt Anym card becomes the dealer for the next round.

Race Day

Skill: matching multiple-meaning words

Number of players: 2–3

Materials:
- enlarged copy of page 88 for each player
- small resealable snack bag for each player
- beanbag for each group
- copy of the key (page 95) for each group

Teacher preparation:
1. Cut apart the word cards from each child's copy of page 88 and store them in a bag.
2. Give each child a copy of the Race Day gameboard and a bag of word cards.
3. Make an enlarged copy of the key on page 95.

Object of the game:

to be the first player to match each word card to its pair of meanings

Playing the game:
1. Each player removes his word cards from his bag and lays them facedown on the playing area near his gameboard.
2. A player places the beanbag between the players.
3. On a start signal, each player silently reads a word card and searches for the strip that shows two meanings for that word. He lays the word card to the left of the matching strip.
4. Players continue the race by reading and matching words until they have placed all of their words.
5. The first player to finish grabs the beanbag. This signals all players to stop.
6. The player who finished first checks the key. If he has all words matched correctly, he wins. If any are incorrect, all players check the key and the player with the most correct answers wins.

©The Education Center, Inc.

Race Day

F. fall	
G. store	
D. bank	
E. trip	
H. tire	
A. play	
I. wave	
B. coat	
C. dress	
J. trunk	

1. to drop down — a season
2. to put away — a place to buy things
3. the slope of a hill — a place to keep money
4. to stumble — a journey
5. to become worn out — a car wheel
6. to take part in a game — a show put on by actors
7. moving the hand to greet — a swell of moving water in the ocean
8. to cover — a heavy jacket
9. to put on clothes — a girl's outfit
10. the stem of a tree — an elephant's nose

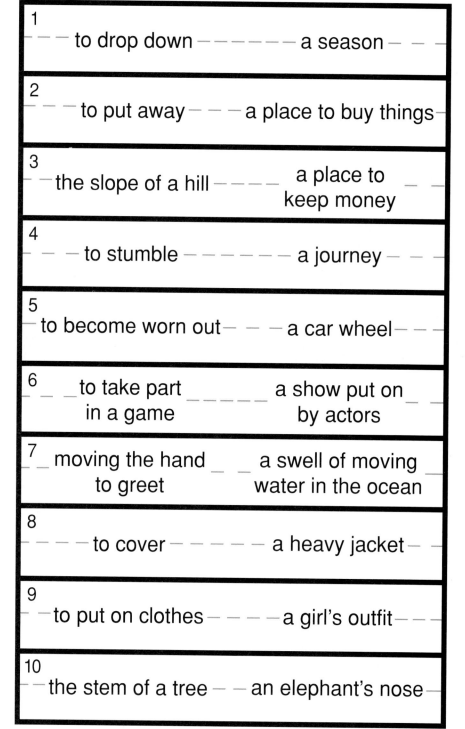

Multiple-Meaning Munchers

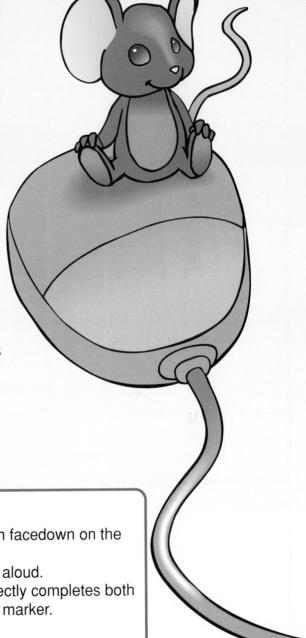

Skill: using homonyms

Number of players: 2

Materials for each player:
- gameboard and game cards (page 90)
- 9 game markers

Teacher preparation:

Cut out a gameboard and a set of game cards for each player.

Object of the game:

to mark one row (of three) on a gameboard, either across or down

Playing the game:
1. Each player stacks her game cards and places them facedown on the playing surface beside her gameboard.
2. Player 1 draws a card and reads the two sentences aloud.
3. Player 1 finds the word on her gameboard that correctly completes both of the sentences. She marks that word with a game marker.
4. Player 2 takes a turn in the same manner.
5. The winner is the first player to mark three words in a row, either across or down, on her gameboard.

©The Education Center, Inc.

Variation:

To give younger students a rhyming word challenge, program each of nine cards with one of the following words: house, vine, rat, tell, tears, soot, rail, far, and brick. Stack the cards facedown between the players and play as directed above.

Multiple-Meaning Munchers

Player _____

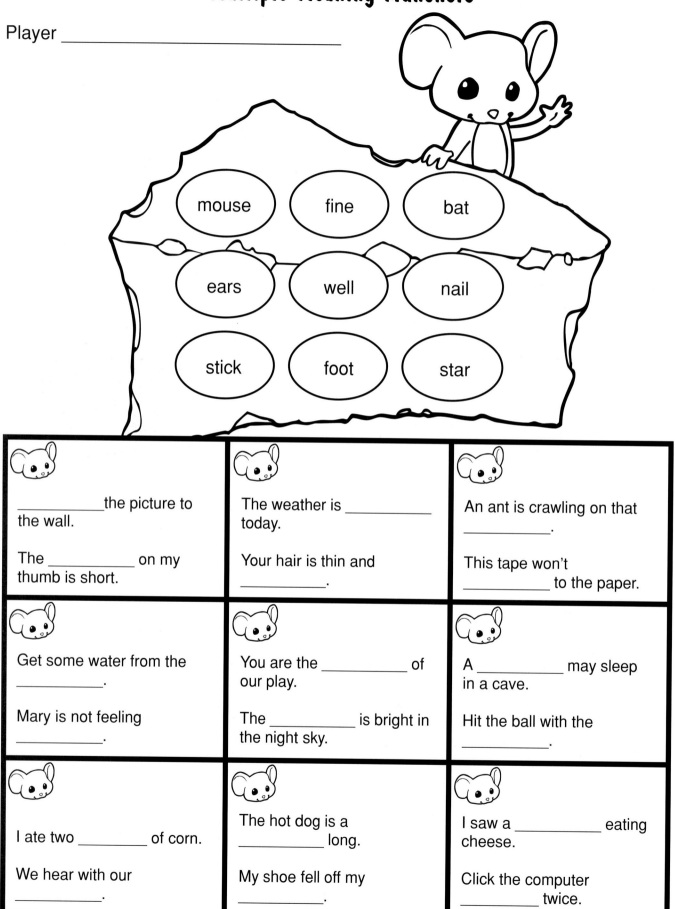

mouse	fine	bat
ears	well	nail
stick	foot	star

_____ the picture to the wall.

The _____ on my thumb is short.

The weather is _____ today.

Your hair is thin and _____.

An ant is crawling on that _____.

This tape won't _____ to the paper.

Get some water from the _____.

Mary is not feeling _____.

You are the _____ of our play.

The _____ is bright in the night sky.

A _____ may sleep in a cave.

Hit the ball with the _____.

I ate two _____ of corn.

We hear with our _____.

The hot dog is a _____ long.

My shoe fell off my _____.

I saw a _____ eating cheese.

Click the computer _____ twice.

Cloudy Contractions

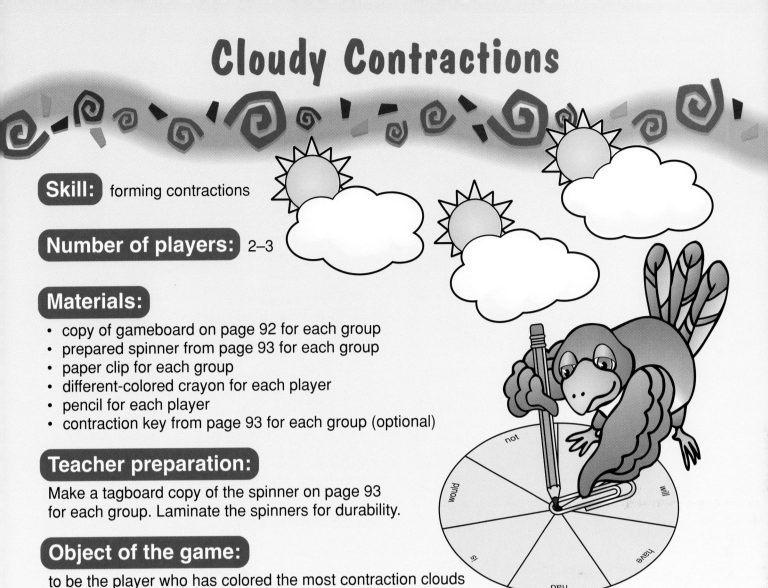

Skill: forming contractions

Number of players: 2–3

Materials:
- copy of gameboard on page 92 for each group
- prepared spinner from page 93 for each group
- paper clip for each group
- different-colored crayon for each player
- pencil for each player
- contraction key from page 93 for each group (optional)

Teacher preparation:

Make a tagboard copy of the spinner on page 93 for each group. Laminate the spinners for durability.

Object of the game:

to be the player who has colored the most contraction clouds

Playing the game:

1. At the top of the gameboard, each player writes his name and colors the cloud next to it to show his game color.
2. Player 1 uses a paper clip and a pencil to spin the spinner and reads aloud the word it lands on. Then he looks at the gameboard to find a word he can combine with the spinner word to form a contraction. If he cannot make a contraction, his turn is over.
3. If Player 1 does find a word to combine with the spinner word to form a contraction, he uses a pencil to correctly write the contraction on the cloud beside the word.
4. If players agree that the contraction is correct, Player 1 uses his crayon to color the cloud. If the players disagree, they check the contraction key or a dictionary. If the contraction is incorrect, Player 1 erases it, and his turn is over.
5. Players 2 and 3 take turns in the same manner.
6. Players take turns until all the clouds are colored. The winner is the player who has colored the most clouds.

Player 1 _____ Player 2 _____ Player 3 _____

Cloudy Contractions

were

who

have

I

are

she

he

they

will

does

can

we

did

you

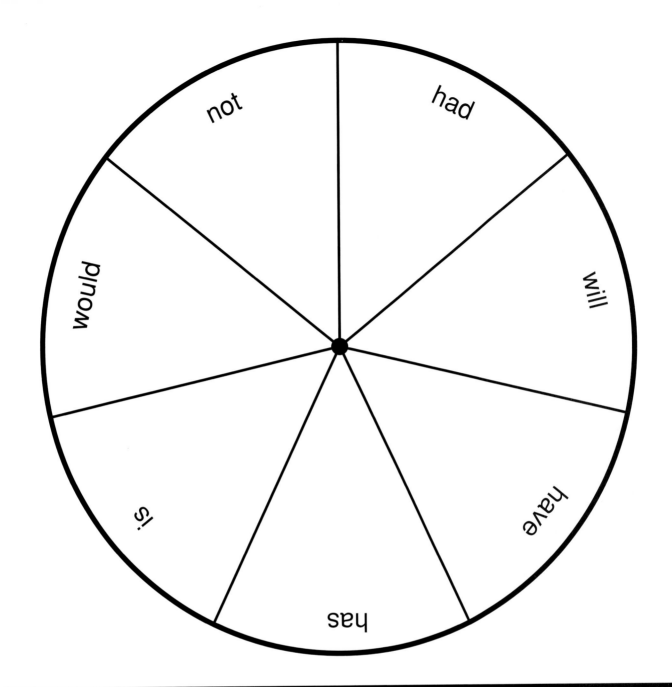

Contraction Key

weren't (were not)
I'd (I would, I had)
I'll (I will)
I've (I have)
she'd (she would, she had)
she'll (she will)
she's (she is, she has)
won't (will not)
we'd (we would, we had)
we'll (we will)
we've (we have)

haven't (have not)
he'd (he would, he had)
he'll (he will)
he's (he has, he is)
doesn't (does not)
didn't (did not)
who's (who is, who has)
who'll (who will)
who'd (who would, who had)
who've (who have)

aren't (are not)
they'd (they would, they had)
they'll (they will)
they've (they have)
can't (can not)
you'd (you would, you had)
you'll (you will)
you've (you have)

Contraction Action

Skill: recognizing contractions and their word sets

Number of players: whole class

Materials:
- newspaper or magazine page
- crayon or marker

Teacher preparation:
1. Separate magazines or newspapers into individual pages. Provide one page for each player.
2. Divide the class into two teams.

Object of the game:
to earn more points by finding contractions or their word sets in reading selections

Playing the game:
1. The teacher calls out a contraction or two words that can be made into a contraction.
2. Players scan their text to find the matching two-word set or contraction. When a player finds a match, she circles it and calls it out. The first player to locate a correct match wins a point for her team.
3. The team with more points at the end of the allotted time wins the game.

©The Education Center, Inc.

Variation:

Have each player being scanning her paper for contractions, circling them as they are discovered. At your signal, have all players stop and count the circled contractions. To claim a win, the player who has the most must name the two-word sets for at least five of her contractions.

Answer Keys

Page 24: "Ski Mt. Syllable"

1. hot
2. basketball
3. vacation
4. ocean
5. butterfly
6. glasses
7. quiet
8. Washington
9. boot
10. December
11. soccer
12. evening or morning
13. kangaroo
14. slow
15. Saturday
16. ketchup
17. igloo
18. attic
19. downhill

Page 32: "Noun Town"

1. snowman
2. teacher
3. forest
4. thread
5. fireman
6. woman
7. fairgrounds
8. desk
9. Mr. Lee
10. mountains
11. bird
12. home
13. mother
14. crayon
15. jungle
16. Dr. Kay
17. suitcase
18. beach
19. boy
20. bottle
21. school
22. hospital
23. hammer
24. classroom
25. child

Page 37: "Treasure Chest of Pronouns"

1. it
2. she
3. it
4. we
5. she
6. they
7. we
8. it
9. it
10. they
11. it
12. he
13. it
14. they
15. we
16. he
17. she
18. it
19. he
20. he
21. we
22. it
23. they
24. it
25. they
26. he
27. they
28. she
29. he
30. he
31. it
32. it
33. they
34. it
35. she
36. she
37. they
38. we
39. she
40. she
41. it
42. she
43. they
44. he
45. we
46. they
47. he
48. they
49. he
50. it

Page 54: "Fiddle-Dee-Dee, We Agree!"

1. am
2. was
3. is
4. was
5. are
6. were
7. are
8. were
9. are
10. were or are
11. Are
12. Were
13. is
14. was
15. is
16. was
17. Is
18. Was
19. is
20. was

Page 56: "All About Adjectives"

1. crisp
2. bumpy
3. three
4. brown
5. salty
6. colorful
7. tall
8. blue
9. thick
10. four
11. shiny
12. large
13. big
14. spotted
15. hot
16. green
17. unhappy
18. fluffy
19. jolly
20. loud

Page 88: "Race Day"

1. F
2. G
3. D
4. E
5. H
6. A
7. I
8. B
9. C
10. J

Project Managers: Hope H. Taylor, Susan Walker
Staff Editors: Denine T. Carter, Diane F. McGraw, Deborah G. Swider
Contributing Writers: Amy Barsanti, Darcy Brown, Lisa Buchholz, Vicki Mockaitis Dabrowka, Josephine Flammer, Heather Graley, Julie Granchelli, Kish L. Harris, Lucia Kemp Henry, Cynthia Holcomb, Cynthia Holzschuher, Lisa K. Jennings, Linda Masternak Justice, Shelly Lanier, Michelle McCormick, Brandi Nash, Leigh Anne Rhodes, Sheryl Romasco, Kelly Wade
Copy Editors: Sylvan Allen, Gina Farago, Karen Brewer Grossman, Karen L. Huffman, Amy Kirtley-Hill, Debbie Shoffner
Cover Artists: Nick Greenwood, Clevell Harris
Art Coordinator: Barry Slate
Artists: Pam Crane, Theresa Lewis Goode, Nick Greenwood, Clevell Harris, Sheila Krill, Clint Moore, Greg D. Rieves, Rebecca Saunders, Barry Slate, Donna K. Teal
Typesetters: Lynette Dickerson, Mark Rainey

President, The Mailbox Book Company™: Joseph C. Bucci
Director of Book Planning and Development: Chris Poindexter
Book Development Managers: Stephen Levy, Elizabeth H. Lindsay, Thad McLaurin, Susan Walker
Curriculum Director: Karen P. Shelton
Traffic Manager: Lisa K. Pitts
Librarian: Dorothy C. McKinney
Editorial and Freelance Management: Karen A. Brudnak
Editorial Training: Irving P. Crump
Editorial Assistants: Terrie Head, Hope Rodgers, Jan E. Witcher